MW01469414

Decluttering Made Simple for Everyone

Strategies to Simplify Your Living Space

Table of Contents

Chapter 1

Understanding Clutter and Its Impact

Clutter is a concept that extends beyond mere disarray; it permeates various areas of our lives, impacting not only our physical surroundings but also our mental and digital spaces. Understanding the complexities of clutter requires a broad perspective, taking into account the ways it infiltrates different facets of existence. Clutter manifests as the accumulation of items that complicate our environments, both visible and invisible. It is not just about tidying up but recognizing how these unorganized elements can lead to stress and create obstacles in our daily routines. By examining the broader implications of clutter, we begin to grasp its pervasive nature and the challenges it poses.

In this chapter, readers will delve into the psychological and emotional aspects of clutter, exploring how it affects our mental well-being and emotional health. The discussion will cover various types of clutter, from the tangible messes that accumulate in our homes to the digital debris lurking in our devices and the emotional tangles that occupy our minds. As professionals juggle busy schedules, the chapter offers insights into how clutter contributes to stress and diminished focus. Through a narrative journey, readers will uncover strategies for recognizing the origins of clutter and tackling it effectively without becoming overwhelmed. By addressing these issues, the chapter aims to equip readers with practical tools to manage their environments, ultimately leading to improved productivity and a more balanced lifestyle.

Define Clutter and Its Sources

Clutter is a word we often hear, but understanding its multifaceted nature requires us to look at it from various angles. Clutter refers to the accumulation of disorganized items, not only in our physical spaces but also in emotional and digital realms, affecting our daily lives. This phenomenon goes beyond the visible chaos in our homes; it includes unseen burdens that cloud our minds or our digital devices, making it difficult to manage efficiently.

Consider physical clutter, the type most people readily identify. It can encompass anything from clothing we don't wear to old furniture gathering dust. Such items pile up not just from daily living but also from gifts received with good intentions, impulse purchases that lose their appeal over time, or cultural pressures encouraging us to acquire more. For instance, social norms might suggest that having an abundantly furnished home signifies success, pushing people to accumulate items they may not necessarily need or want.

The digital age has introduced new types of clutter, particularly on our smartphones, computers, and online accounts. Digital clutter comprises the endless emails filling inboxes, numerous apps installed but seldom used, and unsorted digital files. This kind of clutter is sneakier because it hides behind screens, yet it hinders productivity just as much as a messy desk would. An overflowing email inbox or a desktop littered with unorganized icons can be just as overwhelming as stacks of paper on a workbench.

Then, there's emotional clutter, which consists of unresolved feelings or negative thought patterns. It might originate from the pressure to maintain certain relationships or from sentimental attachments to items due to memories they evoke. These internalized clutters affect mental clarity and contribute to stress. The emotions tied to various possessions can be powerful, making it difficult to let go of things even when they no longer serve a purpose.

An important aspect of understanding clutter is recognizing how life events naturally lead to increased accumulation. Major transitions such as moving to a new house, starting a family, or experiencing loss can introduce significant changes to one's environment, often resulting in additional possessions. As life evolves, so too does our relationship with our belongings. During these times, items that once seemed essential may no longer align with our current needs or desires.

Furthermore, the value we assign to objects plays a significant role in the cluttering process. Personal perceptions heavily influence whether items are kept or discarded. What one person sees as invaluable might be disposable to someone else. These subjective judgments contribute to the difficulty many face when trying to declutter. Often, a mindset shift is required to detach from material goods and recognize that memories and experiences don't reside solely in objects, but rather within ourselves.

Addressing this challenge involves changing how we perceive clutter and adopting a perspective that prioritizes functionality and emotional well-being over merely holding onto items. It's about realizing that an uncluttered environment fosters tranquility and efficiency, allowing for clearer thinking and more meaningful interactions.

Recognizing clutter's origins helps in tackling it effectively. By identifying where and why it amasses, individuals can begin implementing strategies tailored to mitigating these pressures. For some, this might mean setting boundaries around gift acceptance or limiting shopping excursions based on necessity rather than urge. Others might find benefit in setting aside regular times to organize digital files or practice mindfulness to clear emotional cobwebs.

Assess the Emotional Burden of Clutter

Clutter is more than just an eyesore; it has far-reaching implications on mental health, acting as a significant stressor in our daily lives. For busy professionals struggling with jam-packed schedules, understanding how clutter impacts mental well-being can be a powerful motivator for change. Research underscores that cluttered environments elevate stress levels by overwhelming the senses and hindering productivity, which is essential for maintaining focus and achieving goals.

In today's fast-paced world, where multitasking is often deemed a necessity, clutter presents itself as an unwelcome distraction. The brain's capacity to process information is limited, and when surrounded by disorganized items, it struggles to determine what deserves attention. This constant barrage of visual stimuli demands cognitive energy, leading to impaired decision-making abilities and clouded mental clarity. When you're unable to find important documents or personal effects amidst chaos, the frustration intensifies, further affecting cognitive functions.

Furthermore, clutter leads not only to mental exhaustion but also to emotional fatigue. The consistent need to sort through items, some of which may carry sentimental value, creates a cycle where emotional resources are constantly depleted. This feeling of being emotionally drained stems from a perpetual obligation to manage possessions, leaving little room for relaxation or leisure activities. As the mind becomes overwhelmed, burnout becomes a looming threat.

For many, clutter is accompanied by profound feelings of guilt and shame. These emotions arise from the inability to part with belongings that no longer serve a purpose. Whether it's clothes that don't fit or gadgets now obsolete, each item held onto can symbolize unfulfilled aspirations or past decisions that are difficult to reconcile. The psychological burden of holding onto these possessions complicates efforts to declutter, creating a sense of defeat even before beginning the cleanup process.

Acknowledging these negative emotions tied to clutter is crucial. It's common to see one's living space as a reflection of self-worth, where a cluttered environment might suggest personal failure or a lack of control over one's life. This connection can exacerbate feelings of inadequacy and isolation, especially when clutter prevents people from inviting friends or family into their homes. Such social barriers heighten loneliness, a key factor linked to diminished mental health and well-being.

Evidence indicates that clutter jeopardizes emotional stability by fostering an atmosphere of chaos, rather than one of peace and tranquility. An individual's home should ideally be a sanctuary, a place to unwind and rejuvenate after a demanding day. However, clutter disrupts this harmony, transforming spaces meant for rest into sources of agitation. When professionals come home to disorder instead of a calming environment, it negatively affects their ability to relax and recharge for the challenges ahead.

Professionals often find themselves caught in a loop where the time spent managing clutter detracts from more meaningful pursuits. Instead of pursuing hobbies or spending quality time with loved ones, precious hours are lost organizing and reorganizing items. Clutter thus imposes a hidden cost on both time and energy, elements already in short supply for those balancing work pressures and personal commitments.

The narrative surrounding clutter and its impact on mental health isn't just about tidying up physical spaces. It extends to recognizing the psychological toll excess belongings impose and taking actionable steps to address it. By confronting the clutter, individuals can reclaim not only physical space but also mental peace. This process involves shifting perspectives on material possessions, focusing less on accumulation and more on cultivating environments that align with personal values and desired lifestyles.

Ultimately, understanding how clutter undermines mental well-being serves as motivation for change— a call to transform chaotic environments into serene, ordered spaces that support rather than hinder mental and emotional health. Professionals who embrace this mindset can cultivate environments conducive to productivity and happiness, breaking free from the constraints of clutter and moving towards a more balanced, fulfilling way of life.

Recognizing clutter's impact empowers individuals to implement strategies for organization that aren't overwhelming but integrate seamlessly into daily routines. These strategies could involve setting small, manageable goals such as sorting through a single drawer or dedicating ten minutes each day to tidying up specific areas. Over time, these incremental changes build momentum, making the daunting task of decluttering appear more achievable.

Incorporating mindfulness techniques during decluttering sessions can also be beneficial. Approaching the decluttering process with a calm, focused mind allows individuals to make clear-headed decisions about what to keep and what to discard. This practice not only enhances the effectiveness of decluttering efforts but also supports overall mental health by reducing stress and improving emotional resilience.

Embracing a minimalist approach to life, where the emphasis is placed on quality over quantity, can lead to more purposeful living. This means consciously choosing to surround oneself with objects that add genuine value while letting go of items that no longer serve a constructive role. Redefining our relationship with possessions fosters a greater sense of freedom and control, enabling us to create environments that nurture rather than stifle our well-being.

Examine the Time Cost of Maintaining Clutter

Clutter is more than just a visual nuisance; it has profound hidden time costs that can hinder productivity and efficiency in our daily lives. Understanding these time-related challenges can help busy professionals find ways to streamline their environments and reclaim valuable hours.

One major time cost associated with clutter arises from the constant search for misplaced items.

Imagine a typical morning rush when you're frantically looking for your car keys or an important document buried under piles of papers. This scenario, often repeated in cluttered spaces, exemplifies how disorganization consumes precious minutes that could be better spent on productive tasks. A streamlined environment, conversely, ensures that everything has its place, significantly reducing the time required to locate necessary items.

The issue extends beyond personal possessions to affect household chores. Clutter necessitates increased housework, creating a never-ending cycle of cleaning and organizing. Dusting becomes a more laborious task as surfaces are laden with items that need rearranging before they can be cleaned. Similarly, the need to tidy up frequently results in continuous disruption, requiring individuals to spend more time maintaining their living spaces instead of enjoying them. By adopting effective organizational strategies, one can reduce the frequency and intensity of such maintenance efforts, freeing up time for other priorities.

Excessive possessions not only add to the physical burden but also complicate decision-making processes, further prolonging the clutter management ordeal. When surrounded by numerous options, simple decisions become overwhelming.

Whether it's choosing an outfit from an overflowing wardrobe or selecting items to keep or discard, the sheer volume of choices can lead to decision paralysis. Simplifying environments by decluttering can ease this mental load, enabling swifter and more confident decisions.

In addition to these immediate impacts, clutter disrupts responsibilities, leading to routine inefficiencies and resultant time losses. For instance, managing bills and paperwork in a cluttered home office can result in missed deadlines and late payments. These oversights not only consume additional time for rectification but also contribute to stress and financial penalties. Establishing organized systems for handling essential tasks can mitigate such risks and improve overall productivity.

Addressing clutter involves more than just tidying up; it requires a strategic approach to identify and eliminate the root causes of disorganization. Here, guidelines tailored to individual needs can be instrumental. Begin by determining your personal clutter pain points. Is it the pile of unread magazines on your coffee table or the avalanche of clothing spilling out of your closet? Identifying specific areas of concern allows you to tackle them systematically.

Next, set short-term and long-term decluttering goals. Perhaps start with a manageable target, like organizing one drawer or shelf per week, gradually progressing to larger projects over time. Breaking down the process into achievable steps prevents overwhelm and fosters a sense of accomplishment.

Tracking progress with measurable benchmarks adds an element of accountability, making it easier to stay on course. Consider maintaining a decluttering journal where you record areas addressed, items discarded, or time saved. Such tangible records serve as motivation and provide a clear picture of the gains made through sustained efforts.

Finally, celebrate small wins to stay motivated. Recognize the satisfaction of a well-organized kitchen or a clutter-free work desk. Take pride in each step forward, no matter how minor it seems. Positive reinforcement encourages continued commitment to maintaining order.

Summary and Reflections

Throughout this chapter, we have delved into the various dimensions of clutter, examining its sources and the profound psychological and emotional effects it can have. We've explored how clutter extends beyond physical spaces, infiltrating digital and emotional realms, impacting mental clarity and well-being. By understanding the origins and consequences of clutter, individuals are better equipped to confront these hidden burdens that often accompany busy lives. This recognition empowers professionals to take proactive steps in managing their environments, thereby reducing stress and enhancing their overall quality of life.

As busy professionals with demanding schedules, acknowledging the toll clutter takes on our time and mental health is essential for achieving a balanced lifestyle. Clutter not only interrupts productivity but also detracts from the mental space needed for relaxation and personal growth. By addressing these challenges and embracing strategies that integrate seamlessly into daily routines, individuals can create more organized and peaceful living spaces. In doing so, they reclaim their time and energy, fostering environments that support both professional ambitions and personal happiness.

Reference List

Clutter Costs | All Clear Clean Out & Junk Removal Services . (2023, October 4). Www.allclearcleanout.com. https://www.allclearcleanout.com/the-hidden-costs-of-clutter

Fuller, K. (2023, August 21). *How clutter and mental health are connected* . Verywell Mind. https://www.verywellmind.com/decluttering-our-house-to-cleanse-our-minds-5101511

LittleHomeOrganised. (2019, August 21). *Little Miss Organised* . Little Home Organised. https://www.littlehomeorganised.com.au/clutter-meaning/

Massive Psychological Effects Of Clutter, According To Science . (n.d.). Www.miadanielle.com. https://www.miadanielle.com/blog/psychological-effects-of-clutter

Spencer, J. (2023, August). *The Hidden Costs Of Office Clutter: A Comprehensive Analysis For Business Owners - Corporate Vision Magazine* . Corporate Vision Magazine. https://www.corporatevision-news.com/the-hidden-costs-of-office-clutter-a-comprehensive-analysis-for-business-owners/

There are 5 kinds of clutter — which one is filling your life? (2021, April 12). Ideas.ted.com. https://ideas.ted.com/5-kinds-of-clutter/

Chapter 2

Setting Decluttering Goals

Setting decluttering goals involves a strategic approach to transforming a cluttered environment into a more organized and serene space. For busy professionals balancing demanding work schedules, the challenge of managing personal spaces often feels overwhelming. Yet, by establishing clear and realistic objectives, the task transforms from a daunting chore into a structured endeavor. Outlining these goals is akin to charting a course on a map: it provides direction and clarity in what can otherwise seem like an endless sea of clutter. When you have specific goals, such as deciding to rid your living room of unnecessary items by month's end or to finally tackle that burgeoning closet, the process becomes not only manageable but rewarding. Keeping your goals specific allows for a focused effort, turning each step into a marker of progress and encouraging a sense of accomplishment with each milestone reached.

Within this chapter, readers will dive into the techniques of setting effective short-term and long-term decluttering goals. The discussion uncovers how defining particular goals lays the foundation for achieving desired outcomes in a way that aligns with one's routine and lifestyle demands. You'll explore the benefits of breaking down larger projects into smaller, actionable tasks, which minimizes overwhelm and facilitates consistent strides toward completion. Prioritization emerges as a crucial element, urging you to focus energy on areas that yield the most significant impact on daily life or emotional well-being. This section also highlights the importance of setting timeframes to steer clear of procrastination, enabling persistent progress. By weaving these insights together, the chapter equips you with the strategies to navigate decluttering with purpose and precision, making way for a more harmonious living environment that supports your bustling professional life.

Determine Your Personal Clutter Pain Points

In the rush of daily life, it's easy for clutter to creep into our living spaces. Often, busy professionals find themselves overwhelmed by the accumulation of items that seem to appear almost magically. Identifying specific clutter issues is crucial as it allows for focused efforts on areas that genuinely need attention. By prioritizing these areas, you can streamline your decluttering process effectively.

The first step is to identify clutter hotspots within your home. These are specific areas where clutter tends to accumulate over time, such as kitchen counters piled with mail, clothes strewn across the bedroom floor, or entryways littered with bags and shoes. By determining which spots are prone to gathering clutter, you can prioritize where to begin your efforts. An effective method to pinpoint these hotspots is to take photos of each room and review them with fresh eyes, as suggested by professional organizer Diane Quintana (Dyson, 2024). Photos can reveal clutter that has become invisible in day-to-day life. Once identified, dedicate specific time to tackle these areas, making sure they align with your available schedule.

Reflecting on emotional attachment to items is another important step. Emotional ties often hinder our ability to clear out unnecessary possessions, as these objects may be linked to memories or milestones. Understanding why you hold onto certain items can provide clarity and aid in the decluttering process. Take a moment to ponder the significance of each item. This reflection doesn't require an immediate decision but encourages awareness of why certain things hold value. If deeper emotional reasons emerge, consider seeking support, possibly from a therapist, to explore these attachments further (Dyson, 2024). By recognizing the emotional roots behind clutter, releasing unneeded items becomes a more conscious and intentional act.

Balancing functionality against sentimentality is also key in effective decluttering. Ask yourself whether an item serves a practical purpose or merely occupies space due to its sentimental value. For example, keeping a broken appliance because of its nostalgic connection may not justify the space it consumes, especially if it no longer functions. Practical evaluation involves questioning the utility of items: Does this bring convenience or enhance daily life? Does it add unnecessary burden to my living environment? As you weigh these factors, you might find that letting go of some items not only clears physical space but also lightens mental load.

Documenting clutter patterns through a clutter journal is a significant guiding tool. A clutter journal helps track when and where clutter builds up, offering insights into your storage habits and routines. Jot down observations about clutter accumulation trends—are there certain times when clutter spikes, such as after a hectic workweek? Do specific events trigger a lapse in organization? Capturing these patterns enables you to adjust behaviors and implement solutions tailored to your lifestyle. Regularly reviewing your journal provides feedback on progress and reveals persistent issues, allowing for strategic adaptations (Maycroft, 2009). This reflective practice transforms decluttering efforts from sporadic tasks into informed actions backed by personal insights.

While navigating the complexities of clutter, it's essential to implement guidelines that suit your unique circumstances. Create a regular routine for revisiting identified clutter hotspots. Set manageable goals for clearing these areas, pacing yourself to avoid burnout. Awareness of emotional attachments will guide decisions as you consider which items truly belong in your life. Finally, maintain your clutter journal diligently, using it as a living document to evolve your decluttering strategies over time.

Set Short-Term and Long-Term Decluttering Goals

Creating decluttering goals transforms the overwhelming task into a structured and systematic approach. By setting specific goals, you pave the way for a focused and accountable journey through your clutter-filled spaces. Clear objectives serve as a guiding light, keeping you on track and motivated to reach your desired outcome. It becomes easier to visualize what needs to be done, making the once daunting process feel manageable.

To begin, it's essential to define specific goals for your decluttering project. The importance of clear goals cannot be overstated—they provide direction and help keep you accountable. Imagine wanting to tidy up your home; a vague goal like "clean the house" does little to spur action. However, when you set a precise target, such as "clear out unused items from the wardrobe by the end of next week," it injects a sense of purpose and clarity into your efforts. Specific goals delineate boundaries, allowing you to focus attention on particular areas that require hard work (admin, 2024).

Once you've defined specific goals, it's time to break them down into actionable tasks. Large undertakings can feel overwhelming, but by dividing them into smaller, digestible parts, you transform a colossal challenge into a series of manageable actions. Take, for instance, the goal of tackling an overflowing garage. Breaking this into smaller tasks, such as sorting tools, donating old sports equipment, and organizing seasonal decorations, helps streamline the effort. Each small victory propels you forward, creating momentum that builds confidence and keeps discouragement at bay (City, 2024).

Prioritizing your goals based on impact is another crucial step in effective decluttering. Not all tasks carry equal weight or significance, and recognizing this allows for strategic planning. Begin by evaluating which areas or items have the greatest influence on your daily life or emotional well-being. Perhaps the chaotic state of your kitchen counter creates morning stress, or a cluttered office disrupts productivity. By prioritizing these tasks, you ensure that your decluttering efforts yield meaningful improvements. Focusing on high-impact goals maximizes the benefits of your hard work, providing a greater sense of accomplishment and motivation to continue (admin, 2024).

Setting timeframes for achieving your goals is vital. Deadlines instill a sense of urgency, preventing procrastination and helping maintain a steady pace throughout the decluttering process. Without a timeframe, tasks may linger without end, leading to frustration and potential abandonment of the project. Consider establishing mini-deadlines within larger timeframes to create checkpoints along the way. For example, if your overarching goal is to organize the entire living room by the month's end, aim to sort through books one week and tackle electronics the next. These self-imposed deadlines bring structure to your decluttering plan, ensuring continuous progress and preventing the process from stalling (City, 2024).

Implementing these guidelines transforms decluttering from a dreaded chore into a series of achievable steps. With specific goals, each task feels purposeful, and breaking them down removes the intimidation factor associated with large projects. Prioritization ensures that your energy is directed where it counts most, providing immediate relief and satisfaction. Adding timeframes keeps the momentum alive, encouraging consistency and dedication until the finish line is crossed (admin, 2024).

Moreover, envisioning the reward of a clutter-free space can act as powerful motivation throughout the process. Picture yourself walking through an orderly home after completing your decluttering goals—each room serene and free of unnecessary chaos. This vision not only inspires but serves as a constant reminder of why you embarked on this journey in the first place. By visualizing the peaceful haven you're striving to create, you remain committed even during challenging phases of the decluttering endeavor (admin, 2024).

For busy professionals juggling demanding schedules, integrating decluttering into everyday routines may seem impossible. However, by crafting clear, structured goals, the task shifts into something feasible and rewarding. Start small, focusing on specific areas or items, and gradually expand your scope as you gain confidence. Remember, the incremental progress achieved through setting and meeting your goals accumulates over time, ultimately leading to the transformation you desire (City, 2024).

Track Progress with Measurable Benchmarks

Monitoring decluttering efforts is an effective way to maintain consistency and accountability, especially for busy professionals who struggle with organizing due to demanding schedules. The key lies in transforming the process into a routine that integrates seamlessly into daily life. Visual tracking systems, regular checkpoints, public sharing of progress, and reflective reviews all play crucial roles in developing sustainable decluttering habits.

A visual tracking system can become an indispensable tool for anyone looking to stay motivated. By using charts or lists, you gain a tangible representation of your accomplishments. This approach provides instant feedback, highlighting what has been achieved and what still needs attention. For instance, consider maintaining a simple spreadsheet or habit-tracking app where each decluttering task is logged upon completion. Such systems can create a sense of accomplishment as you see tasks checked off, encouraging continued effort. These visuals not only offer motivation but also serve as reminders of your goals, making it easier to stay on track amidst a bustling schedule (Schenkel, 2024).

Incorporating regular checkpoints into your decluttering regimen ensures that you remain accountable and can make strategic adjustments as needed. These checkpoints may be scheduled weekly or monthly, depending on your pace and preference. During these evaluations, assess what progress has been made and identify any obstacles encountered. This practice helps keep momentum going and prevents feeling overwhelmed by large tasks. It allows you to adjust strategies if certain approaches are not yielding desired results. Over time, this habit strengthens your ability to focus and refine your methods, leading to more efficient outcomes (mrpugo, 2023).

Sharing accomplishments with others is another powerful strategy to build encouragement and foster supportive networks around you. Public acknowledgment of your progress can happen through blogging, social media updates, or even discussions with friends or family. When you share your successes, others are likely to cheer you on, providing both moral support and practical advice. Engaging with a community of like-minded individuals can lead to new insights and inspire creative approaches to tackling clutter. Furthermore, sharing milestones publicly can create a sense of accountability, motivating you to follow through on commitments to yourself and others.

Reviewing and reflecting on progress is essential in guiding future strategies and maintaining adaptability. Taking the time to evaluate your successes and mistakes allows you to learn from past experiences and adapt accordingly. Reflective practices could include journaling about what worked well and what didn't during your decluttering sessions. Consider questions such as: What areas were particularly challenging? Were there emotional ties that made letting go difficult? How did overcoming these challenges feel? By analyzing both triumphs and setbacks, you gain valuable insights into personal tendencies and areas needing improvement. This reflection not only fosters growth but also ensures that your decluttering goals evolve alongside changing circumstances and priorities.

Collectively, these strategies form a comprehensive framework for managing clutter effectively. A visual tracking system motivates by vividly displaying achievements, while regular checkpoints provide structured opportunities for evaluation. Sharing your journey with others brings encouragement and accountability, invigorating your resolve. Finally, periodic reflections deepen understanding and direct future action plans.

Wrapping Up

In this chapter, we've explored the vital steps for setting realistic and achievable decluttering goals. By identifying personal clutter pain points, you're able to focus your efforts on troublesome areas that demand immediate attention. Recognizing emotional attachments helps in understanding why we hold onto certain items, which in turn aids in making more conscious decisions when decluttering. We also discussed balancing functionality with sentimentality, ensuring that only truly valuable items remain in your space. Observing clutter patterns through a journal can guide adjustments in habits, making the process more effective. These strategies collectively provide a strong foundation for tackling clutter systematically.

To further streamline your decluttering efforts, setting clear short-term and long-term goals plays a crucial role. Specific objectives help transform the overwhelming task into manageable actions, creating a structured approach that fits into your busy lifestyle. Prioritizing based on impact ensures that essential areas receive focus, thus enhancing daily life significantly. Establishing timeframes injects urgency into the process, helping to maintain momentum and prevent tasks from dragging on indefinitely. By continuously tracking progress and embracing accountability, you foster sustainable habits that lead to lasting change. With these practical tools and insights, decluttering becomes an empowering journey towards a more organized and serene living environment.

Reference List

City. (2024, July 27). *The Ultimate Guide to Decluttering Your Home* . Cityofgoodmaids.com; City of Good Maids. https://www.cityofgoodmaids.com/blog/the-ultimate-guide-to-decluttering-your-home

Dyson, G. (2024, September 3). *What is clutter blindness and how can you fix it? 8 expert steps to help you stop ignoring the mess in your home* . Homesandgardens.com; Homes & Gardens. https://

www.homesandgardens.com/solved/experts-explain-what-clutter-blindness-is-and-how-to-fix-it

Maycroft, N. (2009, November). *Not moving things along: hoarding, clutter and other ambiguous matter* . Journal of Consumer Behaviour. https://doi.org/10.1002/cb.298

Schenkel, J. (2024, May 19). *The Power of Habit Tracking: Conquer Your Goals!* CHANGE JOURNAL. https://changejournal.com/en/blogs/news/habit-tracker?srsltid=AfmBOoonGlfZqTRMY12UC5wH5t6psJ6UiLpdKcTpRd82y-GPODJlTaKl

admin. (2024, February 25). *How to Set Clear Decluttering Goals for a Clutter Free Space - Dare to Declutter* . Dare to Declutter. https://www.daretodeclutter.co.uk/tips/clear-decluttering-goals/

mrpugo. (2023, October 17). *The Importance of Organizing Your Life + Tips for Success - Notion Expert, Digital Creator, YouTuber and Digital Business Nerd* . Pugo\'S Studio. https://pugo.studio/importance-of-organizing-your-life/

Chapter 3

Prioritizing Decluttering Areas

Prioritizing decluttering areas is essential for creating an organized and harmonious home, especially for busy professionals juggling demanding work schedules. When life becomes hectic, the state of our living spaces often mirrors that chaos. A cluttered environment can exacerbate stress and impede productivity, becoming yet another hurdle in the already challenging balancing act between work and personal life. For this reason, identifying and focusing on key areas for decluttering can have a profound impact, not only on the aesthetic appeal of a home but also on one's mental well-being and overall efficiency. By zeroing in on the most utilized spaces, individuals can achieve noticeable results without feeling overwhelmed by the daunting task of organizing an entire house.

In this chapter, you will discover how to assess your living space to identify high-impact areas where decluttering efforts yield significant benefits. The discussion will guide you through practical strategies for breaking down spaces into manageable categories, enabling you to concentrate on areas that directly influence your daily routines. You will learn how to prioritize tasks by assessing clutter levels and understanding the functional importance of each area. Moreover, the chapter delves into the importance of setting realistic time frames for achieving your goals, ensuring that the process remains integrated with your schedule rather than adding to it. The narrative will further explore the balance between short-term wins and long-term organizational goals, empowering you to maintain motivation throughout the decluttering journey. As life changes and priorities shift, you will be equipped with strategies to periodically reassess your plan, adapting to evolving needs while maintaining a clutter-free environment. Through these insights, the chapter aims to provide simple, effective solutions for transforming chaotic spaces into orderly, inviting sanctuaries.

Assess High-Traffic Areas for Immediate Attention

In our daily lives, frequently used spaces hold more power than we may realize in determining the ease and joy of our home environments. Breaking down how to prioritize decluttering these central areas is key to transforming your living space effectively without feeling overwhelmed.

Imagine stepping into your home after a long day. The entryway is the first area you see, setting the tone for your entire dwelling. A cluttered front entrance can create a sense of disarray before you even enter, hindering not just your mood but also the function of the space. By focusing on organizing entryways and hallways, you establish a welcoming atmosphere. Clear pathways free of obstacles enhance navigation, particularly for families with children or elderly members, ensuring smooth movement throughout the house. Additionally, a tidy entrance eliminates stress, making it easier to find keys or bags when rushing out the door. Implementing hooks or a small table for essentials ensures that everything has its place, thus underscoring the importance of organized high-traffic areas. (*The Psychology of Home Design and Decor*, 2024)

The living room, commonly viewed as the heart of a home, serves as a hub for gathering and relaxation. Imagine walking into this space and being greeted by serenity rather than chaos. An orderly living room invites you to unwind, allowing for meaningful conversations and quality time without distractions from clutter. It's here where family bonds strengthen and guests feel comfortable. Maintaining organization within this central environment fosters not only aesthetic appeal but also mental peace. Arranging furniture thoughtfully to encourage open communication and having dedicated spots for remote controls, books, or magazines transforms the living room into a zone of relaxation and happiness.

In modern homes, kitchen counters often fall victim to clutter driven by our fast-paced lifestyles. Consider the impact of walking into a kitchen where countertops are visible and clear. Such an environment inspires a desire to cook and experiment with new recipes, aiding in healthier living habits. With reduced visual noise, meal preparation becomes efficient, encouraging culinary creativity while cutting down on clean-up time. Organizing storage solutions, like using baskets or trays to neatly arrange spices and utensils, enhances functionality and promotes a pleasant cooking experience. Keeping counters clutter-free contributes significantly to smoother daily routines, fueling both productivity and enjoyment in the kitchen.

Turning our attention to workspaces, home offices function as creativity and productivity epicenters, especially for busy professionals. A chaotic office can stifle your ability to focus and create, leading to diminished productivity and elevated stress levels. On the other hand, a well-organized workspace optimizes workflow, minimizing interruptions and distractions. Removing unnecessary materials and arranging important supplies within reach boosts efficiency and creates a conducive environment for innovation. Additionally, personalizing your workspace with meaningful items can foster a positive emotional connection, enhancing motivation and job satisfaction during demanding work schedules (The MOSS Team, 2024).

The choice to declutter and maintain these vital spaces directly influences one's mental health and overall quality of life. Each organized area serves a particular role, collectively contributing to a balanced, harmonious household. By prioritizing high-impact zones, such as entryways, living rooms, kitchens, and home offices, you create a foundation of tranquility that permeates all aspects of your home life.

Adopting practical solutions tailored to each space's needs is crucial. For instance, incorporating built-in cabinetry in entryways efficiently utilizes available space, providing essential storage without overcrowding hallways. Opt for multi-functional furniture pieces in living rooms to maximize usage while keeping surfaces tidy. In kitchens, maintaining minimalism and reducing countertop appliances afford more workspace, while implementing drawer organizers in home offices makes item retrieval straightforward and less time-consuming. Remember, strategically choosing how to organize these critical areas aligns with individual preferences and lifestyle demands, easing everyday tasks while ensuring a lasting, clutter-free environment.

Create a Decluttering Priority List

As busy professionals juggle demanding work schedules with maintaining an organized home, finding a systematic approach to decluttering is essential. Prioritizing decluttering areas begins by breaking down spaces into manageable categories. By assessing the current clutter levels of each area, individuals can determine which spaces impact their daily lives most significantly. For instance, a cluttered kitchen might hinder meal preparation and increase stress during hectic weekdays. Identifying such high-impact areas empowers you to concentrate your efforts where they will make the greatest difference.

Once you've identified key areas, it's crucial to assign realistic time frames for each. This step helps integrate decluttering tasks into your schedule without overwhelming you. Consider how often you use each space and allocate time accordingly. A living room might require more frequent tidying sessions compared to a less-used guest room. Preparing for the decluttering process involves setting aside adequate time, gathering necessary supplies, and even enlisting the help of family members or friends if possible. This collaborative effort not only lightens the workload but also fosters a sense of shared accomplishment.

Setting short-term versus long-term goals is another vital aspect of prioritizing decluttering areas. Short-term goals offer immediate satisfaction and can often be achieved in brief sessions. These might include clearing off a coffee table, organizing a closet shelf, or donating unused items. Achieving these quick wins motivates you to tackle larger projects gradually. Long-term goals, on the other hand, involve comprehensive rearrangements and can be spread over weeks or months. Such projects might encompass reorganizing storage spaces or redesigning a work-from-home setup for improved functionality.

However, life changes, such as a new job or addition to the family, can shift priorities and require reassessment of your original plan. Periodically revisiting and adjusting your decluttering strategy ensures that it remains effective and relevant. Perhaps your initial focus was on the garage, but now that summer is approaching, the backyard may take precedence for social gatherings. Adaptability is crucial to maintaining momentum and preventing frustration when circumstances evolve.

To further enhance your decluttering strategy's effectiveness, consider creating a priority list. Start by categorizing areas based on their function and frequency of use. Kitchens, bathrooms, and living rooms typically demand regular attention due to daily activities, while storage areas like basements or attics may require periodic assessment. This methodical breakdown allows you to systematically address different parts of your home without feeling overwhelmed.

Incorporating time estimates for each area into your priority list adds structure to your cleaning schedule. By knowing approximately how long each task will take, you're better equipped to fit decluttering sessions into your day. Busy mornings could accommodate a 15-minute tidy-up in the entranceway, while weekends might allow for more extensive undertakings in underutilized rooms.

Moreover, distinguishing between short-term and long-term projects in your priority list aids in balancing immediate needs with future aspirations. Quick, satisfying tasks keep you engaged and motivated, whereas longer-term objectives require patience and offer opportunities for creativity. This holistic approach accommodates both immediate improvements and significant organizational transformations over time.

Finally, regular reviews of your priority list maintain its relevance to your evolving lifestyle. Life events, shifting interests, or seasonal changes might necessitate alterations in your decluttering focus. Scheduling monthly or quarterly check-ins enables you to evaluate what's working well and what adjustments are needed. By aligning your actions with your goals, you ensure that your decluttering efforts remain targeted and meaningful.

Utilize a Room-by-Room Approach

When it comes to decluttering, many busy professionals may feel overwhelmed by the prospect of having to tackle their entire living space at once. To make the task more manageable, a structured method that focuses on one room at a time is particularly effective. This approach reduces the daunting nature of decluttering, allowing you to create a sense of order and accomplishment as each area is transformed into a more functional and inviting space.

A systematic focus means addressing one room thoroughly before moving on to the next. Attempting to multitask across multiple spaces can lead to chaos, leaving tasks unfinished and creating more clutter in the process. By concentrating your efforts on a single room, you're able to pay attention to details, ensure everything has its place, and streamline the environment. For example, if you start with the bedroom, you can sort through clothing, remove unnecessary items, and arrange leftover belongings in a way that benefits daily activities. In this way, each room becomes completed and organized before shifting focus elsewhere (Dziak, 2024).

Establishing a dedicated decluttering rhythm is also critical for maintaining organization. Allocate specific times for each room according to your schedule, making the project both orderly and achievable. Perhaps reserve weekend mornings for this purpose, dedicating each session to a different zone within the room. Over time, these sessions will accumulate and lead to noticeable progress. Begin by breaking down larger areas into smaller segments, such as tackling storage closets, under-bed spaces, or dresser drawers individually. Gradually, the results from these consistent efforts will manifest as you see more clutter-free zones (Saviano, 2024).

Understanding room compatibility goes hand in hand with the concept of enhancing functionality. Logical item storage improves day-to-day interactions within spaces designed for specific purposes. The kitchen, for example, should house cooking utensils and appliances within easy reach to streamline meal preparation. Similarly, create a peaceful atmosphere in the bedroom by ensuring that relaxation aids, such as books or essential oils, are within arm's length while minimizing distractions like electronic devices. Thoughtful placement of items based on usage not only enhances the aesthetic appeal but also boosts efficiency in everyday routines.

Developing a repeatable decluttering routine involves revisiting rooms cyclically to solidify organizational skills and maintain long-term home tidiness. Once an area has been initially decluttered and organized, plan to revisit it after a set period—perhaps every few months—to ensure it remains tidy and aligned with how you use the space. This practice prevents regression into cluttered habits and encourages periodic reassessment of what truly needs to be kept. Moreover, it allows for adjustments if lifestyle changes occur, such as transitioning from remote work back to office commuting, which might affect how certain rooms are utilized.

In addition to the practical benefits, approaching decluttering systematically can also provide psychological advantages. Successfully completing one room at a time offers quick wins that boost motivation and satisfaction. Each finished space creates a visual reminder of progress, reinforcing the value of your efforts and encouraging further action. Moreover, focusing on a small, defined area reduces feelings of being overwhelmed, making the overall endeavor appear less intimidating.

Bringing It All Together

As we navigate the complexities of our daily lives, this chapter has highlighted the importance of focusing on key areas within our homes for maximum impact. By turning attention to high-traffic spaces such as entryways, living rooms, kitchens, and home offices, we can transform our environments into havens of order and tranquility. These areas not only set the tone for our interactions with our living space but also influence our mood, productivity, and overall quality of life. Through practical solutions like decluttering, organizing, and prioritizing these zones, a more harmonious home environment emerges, one that aligns with the demands of busy professional lifestyles.

By adopting a room-by-room approach, we ensure that each space is given the attention it deserves without feeling overwhelmed. This systematic method allows us to create functional, inviting areas that support our day-to-day activities seamlessly. Establishing a regular decluttering rhythm enables long-term maintenance, preventing regression into cluttered habits. As priorities shift, perhaps due to changes in work or family dynamics, revisiting our decluttering strategy ensures it remains effective and relevant. Ultimately, this focus on strategic organization forms the foundation for a balanced and stress-free home life, sustaining both mental peace and physical efficiency amidst the busyness of our schedules.

Reference List

Balancing Priorities: Time Management Inspired by Your Purpose . (2024). Becomebraveenough.com. https://www.becomebraveenough.com/blog/balancing-priorities-time-management-inspired-by-your-purpose

Dziak, J. (2024, August 30). *The Simple Strategy For Decluttering Your Home* . The Peasant's Daughter. https://thepeasantsdaughter.net/how-to-declutter-home/

Moore, C. (2023, August 30). *Decluttering Method: Simple 5 Minute Guide* . Chelsijo.co. https://chelsijo.co/2023/08/30/episode-147-decluttering-method/

Saviano, F. (2024, August 24). *Declutter for Mental Health: Key Benefits | Medium* . Medium; Medium. https://medium.com/@francesco.saviano87/declutter-for-mental-health-key-benefits-af5b4a5a1c0e

The Psychology of Home Design and Decor . (2024). San Rufo Homes | Home Builders in Greater Edmonton. https://sanrufohomes.com/the-psychology-of-home-design-and-decor/

The MOSS Team. (2024, January 31). *Clever Storage Solutions for Homeowners to Maximize Their Space* . Mossbuildinganddesign.com; Moss Building and Design. https://www.mossbuildinganddesign.com/blog/clever-storage-solutions-for-homeowners-to-maximize-their-space

Chapter 4

Time Management for Busy Individuals

Time management is a skill that many busy professionals strive to master, as it holds the key to achieving balance amid demanding schedules. In the whirlwind of daily responsibilities, squeezing in tasks like decluttering can feel overwhelming. Yet, by weaving these tasks into our existing routines, there emerges a potential for creating an organized space without feeling burdened. The art lies not just in finding time but in making time, converting the elusive notion of "free time" into productive pockets. This chapter delves into this delicate dance between managing commitments and making room for personal projects, especially decluttering, which often gets overshadowed by pressing deadlines and meetings. It highlights the idea that effective time management is not about doing more but doing what really matters with the time available.

In this chapter, readers will explore strategies for seamlessly incorporating decluttering activities into their hectic lives. The narrative will guide professionals toward establishing decluttering habits through practical methods such as setting aside specific time slots and leveraging productivity techniques. The discussion includes developing a personalized decluttering calendar and using short bursts of focused activity to maintain momentum without sacrificing important commitments. Furthermore, it emphasizes the role of technological tools in reinforcing consistency and accountability. The chapter will also touch on identifying and utilizing downtime effectively, turning otherwise idle moments into opportunities for small, impactful tasks. By focusing on actionable insights, the chapter aims to empower readers to view decluttering not as a daunting obligation, but rather an achievable part of their routine, adding structure and order to their environment while fostering a sense of accomplishment.

Set Aside Specific Time Slots for Decluttering

Incorporating decluttering into the busy schedules of professionals can seem like a daunting task. However, by dedicating specific time slots for these activities, it becomes far more manageable and even less overwhelming. The key here lies in integrating decluttering seamlessly into your already existing routines, thereby making it a consistent habit that does not feel burdensome.

One effective approach to achieving this integration is through the creation of a decluttering calendar. This tool serves as a guide, helping you allocate specific times for decluttering amid your other commitments. By setting aside designated slots, perhaps weekly or bi-weekly, you create a sense of responsibility towards the task, similar to any other appointment or meeting. This consistency is vital, as it forms the foundation of habit formation, allowing decluttering to become a regular part of your life rather than an occasional chore.

To further maximize efficiency, breaking decluttering tasks into short, focused intervals, such as 10-15 minutes, can be incredibly beneficial. Such brief periods prevent feelings of being overwhelmed and help maintain momentum. For instance, instead of allocating a whole afternoon to clear out a room, dedicate a quarter-hour each day to work on a specific section. You may focus on one drawer today and a shelf tomorrow. Over time, these small efforts accumulate, leading to significant progress without causing disruption to your daily routine (mrpugo, 2023).

Moreover, designating certain days exclusively for decluttering can aid in establishing a mental framework that combats procrastination and aligns with your personal productivity cycle. Just as some people are more productive in the mornings or find energy peaks at different times during the week, synchronizing your decluttering efforts with these natural cycles can enhance effectiveness. Consistency in choosing a specific day or set of days also reduces the decision-making burden, ensuring that decluttering doesn't slip through the cracks amid a hectic schedule.

Finally, technology can be an ally in maintaining decluttering habits, with reminders fostering urgency and breaking down resistance. Setting alarms or notifications on your devices can serve as gentle nudges, reminding you of your commitment to declutter. These technological interventions help weave decluttering into your daily routines smoothly, encouraging persistence in tackling cluttered spaces. Apps designed for setting goals and tracking progress can also provide a visual aid, allowing you to see how far you've come and how much is left to achieve (Ceresnak, 2024).

Creating a decluttering calendar starts with identifying the areas in need of attention and then spreading the tasks across your calendar. Choose time frames that naturally fit within your daily rhythm, such as after breakfast or before unwinding in the evening. Including buffer times around your decluttering sessions ensures that this activity doesn't get overshadowed by other responsibilities or appointments. Remember, success lies in consistency rather than perfection, so boxes for missed dates shouldn't deter you but rather encourage flexibility and resilience.

When employing short intervals, consider your energy levels and available time. Perhaps post-lunch breaks or early morning slots work better for you personally. These micro-sessions can be surprisingly powerful. Not only do they capitalize on moments of higher concentration and energy, but they also reduce the hesitance often associated with starting large projects. As you gradually tick off sections of your space over several days or weeks, you'll notice a growing sense of achievement and reduced stress linked with clutter.

Setting specific days for decluttering ties closely to psychological motivation. Knowing that Monday evenings or Saturday afternoons are reserved for organizing can shift your mindset, transforming what might once have felt like a tedious obligation into a structured event. It no longer competes with other priorities because it's carved out as an important, regular duty. This approach helps minimize last-minute scrambles to tidy up before guests arrive or when switching between seasons, facilitating a smoother, more organized lifestyle continuously.

In leveraging technology, various applications can support decluttering endeavors. Calendar apps like Google Calendar or specialized ones like Trello or Asana enable users to plan, track, and structure their decluttering process with reminders and checklists. Furthermore, taking pictures of areas before and after can provide additional gratification, incentivizing further progression. Tech reminders act almost like accountability partners, offering consistent encouragement to push past inertia and face the mess boldly.

Use Productivity Techniques to Maximize Time

In the hustle and bustle of a busy life, finding time to declutter can seem like an insurmountable task. However, integrating productivity methods into decluttering efforts can transform this overwhelming chore into a manageable and even enjoyable activity. One such method is the Pomodoro Technique, which involves breaking work into timed intervals, traditionally 25 minutes in length, with short breaks in between. This technique helps maintain motivation and prevent burnout by making tasks appear less daunting and more achievable. For busy professionals, it offers a structured yet flexible way to incorporate decluttering into their hectic schedules without feeling overwhelmed.

Implementing the Pomodoro Technique for decluttering not only increases focus but also boosts efficiency. By allocating specific bursts of time solely for decluttering, individuals can hone in on the task at hand instead of getting sidetracked by other responsibilities or distractions. What makes this method particularly effective is its ability to break down large decluttering projects into manageable segments. Instead of viewing decluttering as an all-day affair, it becomes a series of short, focused sessions that fit comfortably within a busy schedule. Moreover, frequent breaks help replenish mental energy, ensuring sustained productivity over longer periods.

Batching similar tasks is another powerful strategy that benefits those looking to declutter effectively. By grouping similar items or areas for decluttering, you minimize the time lost transitioning between different types of activities. For instance, spending one session sorting through clothes and another dedicated to sorting books can create a more fluid workflow. Reducing the cognitive load associated with constant switching allows you to remain immersed in a single type of task, thereby conserving valuable time and energy (Silvestre, 2020). This approach aligns well with the fast-paced lives of busy professionals by promoting a sense of accomplishment with each completed batch.

Setting time limits on tasks is crucial for maintaining a balance between decluttering and other daily obligations. Establishing a predetermined amount of time for each decluttering session encourages sharper decision-making and enhances focus. The pressure of a ticking clock often fosters a greater sense of urgency, motivating individuals to stay concentrated and complete more within the allotted time. This focus can lead to quicker yet efficient decision making about what items to keep, donate, or discard.

Using a timer during decluttering sessions not only improves accountability but also adds an element of fun. It transforms the process into a challenge against oneself—seeing how much can be accomplished before the timer signals the end. Timers serve as tangible markers of progress, providing immediate feedback on how much has been achieved in a given period. This gamified aspect can make decluttering less of a chore and more of an engaging activity. Furthermore, consistently using a timer helps develop a rhythm and routine, making it easier to slot decluttering tasks into even the busiest of days.

Leverage Downtime for Small Tasks

In our bustling world, time is often seen as the most precious commodity. For busy professionals striving to maintain an organized living space amidst demanding schedules, every minute counts. Embracing moments of downtime to address smaller decluttering tasks can lead to significant benefits without requiring substantial investments of time or energy.

Recognizing unused fragments of time in your daily schedule can transform them into opportunities for small yet impactful actions. Imagine standing by the microwave waiting for your lunch to heat or having a brief moment between meetings. These instances are often dismissed as mere gaps, but they hold potential when leveraged wisely. Identifying these down moments shifts the mindset from reactive to proactive, allowing individuals to take action without compromising their main tasks (Monroe, 2024).

Creating a list of quick decluttering tasks can serve as a powerful tool in this endeavor. Jotting down simple tasks like organizing a drawer, sorting through a stack of mail, or clearing out old digital files on your phone can make decision-making effortless when time arises. By reducing decision fatigue, a well-prepared list encourages incremental progress and keeps motivation high. The sense of accomplishment gained from ticking off small tasks provides positive reinforcement, driving further productivity throughout the day.

Every mundane activity holds the potential for multitasking in a non-overwhelming way. Waiting in line, riding the elevator, or sitting in traffic can become opportunities for mental decluttering or planning future tasks. For instance, while waiting at the doctor's office, you could brainstorm ideas for better organization in your home or identify items that need disposing of. This approach significantly enhances productivity during idle times without imposing additional stress (Kurtz, 2023).

Decluttering isn't just about physical spaces; it involves a mental shift toward mindfulness. Engaging thoughtfully in even the smallest decluttering activity can convert these tasks into reflective experiences. As you tidy up a cluttered corner or sort through paperwork, consider how each object contributes to the chaos or harmony of your environment. This mindset fosters a deeper appreciation for your surroundings and highlights the importance of maintaining order and balance in everyday life.

Consider the method of scheduling bulk sessions as viable support for tackling larger decluttering projects. Allocating specific periods for more intensive efforts complements the ongoing practice of utilizing downtime for swift tasks. It creates a harmonious routine where progress is consistently made, both in smaller bursts and focused intervals (Monroe, 2024).

Inviting family members to join decluttering activities transforms them into collaborative ventures. By sharing responsibilities, household members not only accomplish tasks faster but also learn valuable organizational skills. This teamwork instills a shared sense of accountability, ensuring continued effort toward maintaining clutter-free spaces.

Establishing clear goals for each decluttering session adds structure to what might initially feel daunting. Clearly defining objectives, whether it's emptying a particular closet or reducing paper clutter, offers direction and motivation. These short-term goals create stepping stones leading to long-term achievements, making the process manageable rather than overwhelming.

Reflective practices during decluttering encourage individuals to reconsider their relationship with possessions. Mindfulness during these tasks develops awareness of what truly matters, aiding in the discernment between necessary and superfluous objects (Kurtz, 2023). This approach amplifies not only organizational efficiency but also personal fulfillment, resulting in an environment that supports well-being and productivity.

For individuals who find themselves perpetually busy, harnessing downtime to accomplish minor decluttering tasks is transformative. It redefines how time is perceived and maximizes output without overextending resources. In doing so, it alleviates the pressure of sustained organization, offering sustainable solutions for a clutter-free living space amid the chaos of demanding schedules.

Bringing It All Together

In this chapter, we explored strategies to seamlessly incorporate decluttering into the busy lives of professionals. By setting aside specific time slots and creating a decluttering calendar, we learned how to make organization a regular part of our routines. Brief, focused intervals help maintain momentum without feeling overwhelmed, while aligning decluttering tasks with natural productivity cycles enhances effectiveness. Technology aids in setting reminders and tracking progress, ensuring that decluttering becomes a consistent habit rather than an occasional chore.

Additionally, we discussed using productivity techniques like the Pomodoro Technique and batching similar tasks to maximize efficiency. Recognizing downtime as opportunities for quick decluttering activities can lead to significant progress over time. Maintaining a balance between larger sessions and minor tasks allows for continuous improvement without disruption. Involving family members and setting clear goals transform decluttering into a shared responsibility. Through mindful practices, we not only organize physical spaces but also foster a greater sense of well-being and productivity in daily life.

Reference List

Ceresnak, R. (2024, April 25). *Integrating Life Hacks for Everyday Productivity and Efficiency* . Medium. https://medium.com/@romanceresnak/integrating-life-hacks-for-everyday-productivity-and-efficiency-4d4fc41d9f09

Demid. (2023, October 19). *Time Management Hacks for Increased Productivity - Demid - Medium* . Medium. https://medium.com/@Anvaerro/time-management-hacks-for-increased-productivity-d790b335b4f4

Kurtz, T. (2023, September 4). *Clean Method* . Clean Method. https://cleanmethod.com/blog/declutter-office-boost-productivity/

Monroe, J. (2024, April 30). *Productive Procrastination: Surprising Benefits (Plus Useful Strategies)* . Usemotion.com. https://www.usemotion.com/blog/productive-procrastination

Silvestre, D. (2020, April 15). *13 Effective Time Management Strategies for Ultimate Focus Dan Silvestre* . Dan Silvestre. https://dansilvestre.com/time-management-strategies/

mrpugo. (2023, October 17). *The Importance of Organizing Your Life + Tips for Success - Notion Expert, Digital Creator, YouTuber and Digital*

Business Nerd . Pugo\'S Studio. https://
pugo.studio/importance-of-organizing-your-life/

Chapter 5

Minimalist Mindset for Sustainable Decluttering

Adopting a minimalist mindset is an ongoing journey toward a more intentional life. For busy professionals juggling endless tasks, this approach can offer a refreshing perspective on managing both personal and professional spaces. Minimalism isn't just about decluttering; it's about making conscious choices to focus on what genuinely matters. This lifestyle encourages individuals to examine their possessions and commitments through a lens of purpose and joy. As you begin to integrate minimalist principles, you'll likely find that your mental clarity improves along with your surroundings. Such clarity allows for better decision-making and reduced stress, providing the breathing room needed to enjoy life's simple pleasures fully.

In this chapter, we delve into the core tenets of minimalism and how they pave the way for sustainable decluttering. You will explore the transformative impact minimalism can have on reducing stress through simplified decision-making processes. We will also discuss the importance of choosing quality over quantity, fostering mindful consumption practices that emphasize needs over wants. The flexibility inherent in adopting a minimalist lifestyle enables you to tailor it according to personal values and priorities. By understanding how to identify essentials versus non-essentials, you can maintain organized living spaces even with demanding schedules. This chapter ultimately aims to provide you with practical insights and strategies for embracing a minimalist mindset, helping you align your environment with your internal values for a more balanced and fulfilling life.

Understanding the Core Tenets of Minimalism

To truly embrace minimalism, one must first understand its fundamental principles. This approach to life emphasizes intentional living by honing in on what genuinely matters. For the busy professional, minimalism can transform not just a physical space but also one's mental landscape.

Imagine starting each day knowing exactly what is necessary. Minimalism encourages you to focus on items that contribute meaningfully to your life. It's about evaluating possessions and commitments with a lens of purpose and joy. Instead of being overwhelmed by things that merely fill space and time, minimalists curate their surroundings to reflect values and aspirations (becker, 2011).

Minimalism significantly reduces stress by simplifying decision-making processes. With fewer possessions, your energy and focus aren't scattered across managing countless items. Imagine opening a closet or drawer where everything serves a purpose, allowing you to start your day without the stress of sifting through clutter. This clarity extends beyond physical spaces to mental ones, freeing up time and energy for what truly matters. In fact, embracing this lifestyle provides the breathing room needed to enjoy existing possessions fully, fostering gratitude and mindfulness rather than endless consumption cycles (No Sidebar, 2024).

Choosing quality over quantity is another key tenet of minimalism. It's about making deliberate choices that enhance daily experiences. This might mean investing in a high-quality coffee maker that delivers the perfect brew every morning, rather than three budget appliances that fall short of expectations. Such intentionality ripples outward into all areas of life, influencing how you allocate your time and resources. By focusing on fewer, better-crafted items, you gain satisfaction from longevity and the absence of constant replacements. This practice aligns with mindful consumption—buying less means waste less, an increasingly important consideration in today's world (No Sidebar, 2024).

The beauty of minimalism lies in its subjectivity; it's a deeply personal experience that enables individuals to align their external environment with internal values. Common misconceptions suggest that minimalism equals deprivation, yet it is quite the opposite. Minimalism allows you to define what is essential and enriching for your unique journey, shedding societal pressures to accumulate more. Think of the professional who finds freedom in a wardrobe of a few favorite outfits rather than an overstuffed closet. This personalized approach helps dismantle the idea that happiness requires material abundance, instead promoting fulfillment derived from relationships, experiences, and personal growth.

In navigating minimalism's principles, there are no rigid rules. Flexibility is inherent to the minimalist mindset, inviting individuals to interpret the philosophy according to personal needs and desires. Pursuing minimalism doesn't render you immune to keeping sentimental items; rather, it allows you to honor these objects' significance without them overshadowing the rest of your life. The minimalist lifestyle demands introspection—an understanding of what we need to live a balanced, intentional life. As you pare down distractions, minimalism facilitates deeper connections and a stronger sense of self-awareness (becker, 2011).

Adopting minimalism could be seen as a radical act in our hyper-consumerist world. It challenges the notion that acquiring more leads to happiness and fulfillment. Minimalism invites a shift in perspective, encouraging us to find satisfaction and contentment within simplicity and sufficiency. This change can cultivate a rewarding life by engaging more with experiences, forging stronger bonds with others, and contributing positively to the community and environment.

While adopting minimalism might seem daunting initially, it is entirely achievable. Begin small, perhaps by decluttering a single room or simplifying a daily routine. As you gradually integrate these principles, you'll likely discover newfound freedom and clarity. Minimalism offers a pathway to reclaim ownership of your time, focus, and energy—a liberation from the frenzy often brought by excessive consumer culture.

As professionals with demanding schedules, integrating minimalism can seamlessly dovetail with personal and career goals. By prioritizing duties and possessions that align with core values, you craft a more manageable and vibrant existence. Harness the minimalist mantra of 'less is more' to alleviate chaos and foster environments where you can thrive.

Embracing Quality Over Quantity

Investing in durable, high-quality items can result in long-term savings and satisfaction. At first glance, the cost of a well-made product might seem like a significant financial commitment. However, this initial expense is often offset by the longevity and durability these items offer, reducing the need for frequent replacements. Consider furniture as an example. While cheaper options may tempt you with their lower prices, they often fail to stand the test of time, leading to repeated purchases and increased costs in the long run. High-quality pieces, on the other hand, are crafted with superior craftsmanship and materials. This careful construction not only provides lasting beauty but also enduring functionality (Heirloom, 2024).

When you start to rethink purchases, consider the importance of thorough research and criteria development before making buying decisions. In our fast-paced world, it's easy to succumb to impulsive buys that clutter our homes without truly serving us. For busy professionals seeking efficient solutions for their living spaces, developing a set of criteria can be especially beneficial. These criteria should reflect personal needs, values, and lifestyle preferences, ensuring that each purchase contributes positively to your life. Before purchasing, ask yourself whether the item meets these criteria. Is it essential? Does it bring joy? Will it last? Research manufacturers, read reviews, and compare products to ensure informed decisions that align with your goals.

Mindful consumption is another aspect of choosing quality over quantity, aligning spending with personal values and emphasizing needs over wants (Wainwright, 2024). Practicing mindfulness when consuming means taking a step back and questioning the purpose behind each purchase. It prioritizes essential items over unnecessary ones, which adds value rather than excess. By being more conscious, individuals can divert resources toward what truly matters—enhancing the quality of their lives and keeping their living spaces organized and free from clutter. Instead of accumulating piles of possessions that hold little meaning, mindful consumption leads to owning fewer but more meaningful and functional items, resulting in a more serene and intentional living environment.

Curating a collection of well-made items enhances home organization and fosters meaningful connections within the space. When you surround yourself with quality items you genuinely appreciate, each piece serves its function and adds to your home's overall aesthetic and atmosphere. This approach nurtures a sense of pride and satisfaction in your surroundings, transforming them into a sanctuary where you feel comforted and inspired. Moreover, fostering a connection with your belongings encourages care and maintenance, further extending their lifespan. For example, a robust dining table isn't just a piece of furniture; it becomes a gathering spot for family dinners and friendly conversations, creating cherished memories over time.

Guidelines for cultivating mindful consumption can be instrumental in assisting those new to this concept. Begin with a simple exercise: identify key areas or categories in your living space that tend to accumulate clutter, such as closets or bookshelves. Evaluate each item carefully, determining its utility and emotional significance. If an object no longer serves a purpose or brings joy, consider donating or recycling it. Establish a habit of regularly assessing these areas to maintain clarity between what is essential and what is superfluous. Additionally, try to apply a "one-in, one-out" rule when introducing new items into your living space. This practice helps ensure that every new addition replaces something else, preventing accumulation and maintaining balance.

In building a quality collection, there are several strategies to explore. Prioritize versatility and multi-functionality, opting for pieces that serve multiple roles, such as furniture with storage capabilities or kitchen gadgets that perform several tasks. Another strategy involves seeking out timeless designs that transcend fleeting trends, ensuring that your items remain relevant and stylish for years to come. Embracing simplicity and clean lines often results in a collection that is both adaptable and aesthetically pleasing.

Furthermore, there's a certain beauty in surrounding ourselves with well-crafted objects that resonate with our personal narratives. Each piece can tell a story, contributing to our home's tapestry.

Emphasizing quality over quantity allows us to cultivate a space that reflects who we are and what we value.

Learning to Identify Essentials Versus Non-Essentials

In the realm of minimalist living, the art of distinguishing between necessary and unnecessary items holds a pivotal role. This skill is essential for busy professionals aiming to maintain organized living spaces despite demanding schedules. Building a sustainable decluttering strategy starts with defining what constitutes an 'essential.' To begin with, essentials are items that either fulfill practical needs or hold significant personal value. Understanding this dual criterion can tremendously simplify the decluttering process.

Consider the countless items you encounter daily. It can be overwhelming to identify what deserves space in your life. Practicality often dictates necessity. For example, a winter coat in a cold climate serves a clear purpose, warranting its place in the closet. On the other hand, items of personal significance might include family heirlooms or reminders of meaningful experiences, such as a souvenir from a memorable trip. These possessions earn their keep due to the joy or comfort they bring, aligning with a minimalist mindset's core principle: only keeping objects that serve a genuine purpose or elicit happiness.

To put this into practice, frameworks such as the 'six-month rule' become invaluable tools. According to this guideline, if an item hasn't been used within the past six months, it's unlikely to be essential. Of course, there are exceptions—seasonal items or emergency supplies might require adjustments to this timeframe. However, this rule generally helps cut through uncertainty, allowing individuals to make more objective decisions about what truly belongs in their lives.

Balancing practicality with personal value demands recognizing and overcoming emotional attachments that often clutter our environments. Emotional attachments can manifest in diverse ways—a gift from someone meaningful, memorabilia from past events, or even items inherited from loved ones. While these objects can evoke nostalgia, differentiating between sentimental value and actual utility is crucial. Ask yourself whether the attachment is rooted in fond memories or a sense of obligation. For instance, holding onto boxes of childhood toys out of guilt might not contribute positively to your current lifestyle. Instead, capturing memories through photographs can preserve those sentiments without occupying physical space.

It's normal for emotional connections to influence our decision-making. However, experts suggest focusing on retaining items that align with present-day priorities. Practicing gratitude towards these objects before releasing them can foster a smoother transition. Imagine gifting a cherished book to a younger relative who shares your literary passion; doing so not only passes along the joy but also frees up space in your own home.

Enabling ongoing clarity between essentials and non-essentials requires integrating regular assessment routines into daily life. Decluttering isn't a one-time task; it's an evolving practice that adapts to changing circumstances and preferences. Conducting periodic reviews of your possessions ensures you remain aligned with your values and goals. A simple approach involves setting aside time each month or season to examine areas prone to clutter accumulation. Closets, junk drawers, and storage rooms are hotspots worth revisiting.

During these assessments, query items with questions such as "Does this still serve a purpose?" or "Does this contribute to my current lifestyle?".

This reflective practice steers focus away from impulsive attachments and towards mindful curation. Moreover, breaking the task into manageable chunks prevents overwhelm, making it feasible for professionals juggling tight schedules.

Establishing a no-clutter zone can significantly reinforce these routines. Designate specific areas in your home where clutter is strictly off-limits, such as bedside tables or workspaces. Having these zones promotes mindfulness and instills habits of tidiness, encouraging individuals to apply the same principles throughout their living spaces.

Reflecting on this journey of distinguishing essentials, it's vital to acknowledge the empowerment minimalism brings. By consciously choosing which items stay and which depart, individuals forge environments conducive to both productivity and tranquility. The simplicity of less ultimately cultivates more space—both physically and mentally—for opportunities and experiences that truly matter.

Insights and Implications

As this chapter draws to a close, we've explored how adopting minimalism can lead to lasting success by simplifying both your physical and mental landscapes. By prioritizing what truly matters and letting go of excess, minimalism allows busy professionals to focus their energy on meaningful aspects of life. This journey begins with evaluating possessions and commitments through a lens of purpose and joy, ultimately reducing stress and enhancing clarity. Choosing quality over quantity fosters mindful consumption, leading to long-term savings and satisfaction. By investing in durable items and rethinking purchasing decisions, you create an environment that aligns with personal values, enhancing the living space's functionality and aesthetics.

The practice of distinguishing between essentials and non-essentials further empowers individuals to maintain organized spaces despite hectic schedules. This involves recognizing what holds practical or personal value while overcoming emotional attachments that contribute to clutter. Regular assessments ensure alignment with your current lifestyle, promoting mindfulness and tidiness across different areas of your home. Minimalism invites you to cultivate environments that reflect who you are, allowing for greater productivity, tranquility, and deeper connections. As a pathway to simplified living, it challenges societal norms of accumulation, offering a liberating choice to prioritize experiences, relationships, and growth over material abundance.

Reference List

Heirloom, in. (2024, August 31). *Wild Edge Woodcraft* . Wild Edge Woodcraft. https://doi.org/103209340/c487c211-c2b3-49d7-bbc4-2621af18d95d

No Sidebar. (2024, May 11). *10 Essential Principles of Minimalist Living* . No Sidebar. https://nosidebar.com/10-essential-principles-of-minimalist-living/

Treading, L. (2016, September). *From Decluttering to Done: can this one step make all the difference?*

Treading My Own Path. https:// treadingmyownpath.com/2016/09/01/from- decluttering-to-done-one-step-that-makes-all-the- difference/

The Happy Philosopher. (2016, May 10). *Decluttering 2.0 – Beyond The Basics* . The Happy Philosopher. https://thehappyphilosopher.com/ decluttering-beyond-the-basics/

Wainwright, A. (2024, February 26). *What Is Product Durability & Why Is It Important? | Zupan* . Zupan.ai. https://zupan.ai/blog/what-is-product- durability

becker, joshua. (2011, June 20). *What Is Minimalism?* Becoming Minimalist. https:// www.becomingminimalist.com/what-is- minimalism/comment-page-4/

Chapter 6

Effective Decluttering Strategies

Reducing clutter in your home is a task that can greatly enhance the quality of your living environment. With demanding schedules and busy lives, many professionals find their homes becoming overwhelmed with items that contribute to stress rather than solace. Decluttering offers not only physical space but also mental clarity, providing a sanctuary from day-to-day pressures. As you navigate through the process, it's essential to consider strategies that are simple yet effective, aligning with your lifestyle needs without adding to your workload.

In this chapter, various decluttering methods tailored for busy individuals are explored. You'll discover how adopting conscious item replacement can create a balanced and sustainable approach to maintaining order at home. By investigating techniques like the 'One In, One Out' rule or conducting regular wardrobe reviews, you'll be equipped with practical tools to make your spaces more organized. The concept extends beyond mere tidying, encouraging a shift in consumption habits towards mindfulness. Additionally, digital decluttering techniques will be addressed, recognizing that an uncluttered digital space contributes as significantly to overall well-being as physical tidiness does. These methods offer achievable steps that fit seamlessly into your routine, transforming the act of decluttering from a daunting chore into an empowering practice.

'One In, One Out' Rule

In the quest for a clutter-free home, one effective strategy is to adopt the practice of conscious item replacement. This approach revolves around the simple rule: every time I introduce a new item into my home, I must remove one that no longer serves a purpose. By doing so, mindful consumption is fostered, and a sustainable cycle of decluttering emerges.

Let's delve deeper into how this method works. When you bring a new pair of shoes into your closet, find an older pair that's worn out or rarely worn, and let it go. If a new book makes its way onto your shelf, consider donating one you've already read. This act of replacement not only prevents unnecessary accumulation but also encourages thoughtful decision-making before each purchase. As we become more deliberate with our buying habits, we start to see shopping as more than just acquiring; it's about curating what we truly need and value.

The benefits of adopting such mindful practices are multifaceted. First, there's a growing sense of relief from stress as spaces remain organized and uncluttered over time. When clutter is minimized, we experience less mental chaos. With fewer items to manage, cleaning becomes quicker and simpler, freeing up precious hours for other activities. Additionally, when everything has its place, there's less anxiety stemming from misplaced belongings. It's refreshing to walk into a room where each possession has been deliberately chosen and placed, creating an environment of calm and clarity.

However, this approach isn't without its challenges. One significant hurdle is emotional attachment to possessions. Many of us hold onto items because they are tied to memories or gifted by loved ones. Parting with them can evoke feelings of disloyalty or loss. Yet, there are strategies to navigate these emotions effectively. Start by acknowledging the memory an item represents and express gratitude for its role in your life. Remember, the value lies in the memory itself, not necessarily in the physical object. This mindset shift can make it easier to let go. Another approach is to repurpose sentimental items. For instance, if an old dress holds special memories but no longer fits, consider turning its fabric into a decorative pillow cover. This not only keeps the item close but gives it renewed usefulness.

As we continue on this path of mindful consumption, we benefit from regular reflection on our possessions, making it a habit to reassess what truly adds value to our lives. Over time, this introspection leads to a living space that's not only physically organized but also brings psychological relief. Our homes become sanctuaries that support relaxation and productivity, rather than sources of stress and disorder.

One practical example to illustrate conscious consumption is conducting seasonal wardrobe reviews. With each new season, assess your clothing collection. Identify pieces that haven't been worn and decide whether to donate, sell, or recycle them. This periodic evaluation ensures that your wardrobe remains relevant, functional, and free of redundancy. Similarly, apply this principle to kitchen gadgets, electronics, and hobby supplies. If a device hasn't been used in recent months, consider its necessity before purchasing something new.

A potential pitfall is impulse shopping, especially when faced with sales or limited-time offers. It's easy to succumb to the allure of discounts, forgetting whether the item is truly needed. To overcome this temptation, maintain a wish list for non-essential purchases. Before buying, check if the item aligns with your existing needs or desires. Evaluate whether it fills a genuine gap or merely satisfies a momentary craving. This approach curbs impulsive decisions and ensures that new acquisitions genuinely contribute to your lifestyle.

Moreover, integrating conscious consumption into daily routines can reinforce positive habits. Whenever you contemplate a purchase, ask yourself: Is there something similar at home I can discard? Where will this new item reside? Such questions not only promote mindfulness but also highlight the importance of maintaining balance in your inventory.

'12-12-12' Method

In our fast-paced lives, maintaining an organized and clutter-free home might seem like an insurmountable challenge. However, by adopting a straightforward method focused on finding 12 items to donate, discard, or relocate in each session, busy professionals can transform their living spaces into serene sanctuaries without overwhelming themselves. This structured approach breaks down the daunting task of decluttering into manageable pieces, allowing anyone to chip away at clutter incrementally.

Picture this: you're standing in your living room, surrounded by items you've accumulated over the years. The thought of sorting through everything is enough to make you want to give up before you've even started. That's where the 12-item method comes in. By choosing just twelve items at a time to either donate, discard, or relocate, the process becomes less intimidating. You focus on small victories, progressively transforming your space with each session. It's not about achieving perfection overnight but fostering consistent progress that fits seamlessly into your schedule.

Integrating decluttering into your daily routine can be surprisingly achievable. Consider those spare moments throughout your day—whether it's a break between meetings or waiting for the kettle to boil. These short bursts of time can become your allies in developing a steady decluttering habit. For instance, dedicate eight minutes each day, as suggested by some decluttering enthusiasts, to focus on specific areas. Perhaps start with your bathroom or workspace, gradually extending to other parts of your home. This strategy ensures that decluttering doesn't disrupt your already packed agenda but instead complements your lifestyle. By seizing these small windows of opportunity, you cultivate a habit that soon becomes second nature.

The psychological benefits of this method extend beyond the physical space it frees. A decluttered environment significantly enhances mental clarity, promoting a clearer focus and positive mindset. Imagine walking into a room where everything has its place, free from extraneous distractions. This orderliness helps reduce stress levels and enhances productivity. You're no longer burdened by visual noise or the nagging thought of tidying up. Instead, your mind is liberated to concentrate on what truly matters.

Real-life success stories further highlight the effectiveness of this method, making it relatable and inspiring for those embarking on their decluttering journeys. Take Sarah, a marketing executive, who transformed her home by dedicating as little as ten minutes daily to the task. Initially skeptical, she found herself looking forward to her decluttering sessions. The changes were subtle yet profound; she experienced reduced anxiety and slept better at night. Sharing her journey with friends on social media, Sarah inspired others to try the method, creating a ripple effect in her community.

Another powerful testimony comes from Tom, a freelance writer, who struggled to find time for decluttering amid project deadlines. He embraced the 12-item method during his lunch breaks. Within weeks, his workspace evolved from chaotic to organized, boosting his creativity and efficiency. By integrating decluttering into his daily rhythm, Tom discovered it wasn't just about tidying up his surroundings but also rejuvenating his mind.

What stands out in these stories is the simplicity and adaptability of the method. It's not prescriptive but flexible, allowing individuals to tailor it to their needs and schedules. Whether tackling a notorious junk drawer or streamlining a wardrobe, the process remains the same—concentration on small, achievable goals leads to significant transformations.

For those ready to embrace this decluttering journey, remember it's about consistency, not speed. Start by identifying 12 items today and continue building momentum with each session. Soon, you'll create an environment that not only looks tidy but supports your well-being.

Digital Decluttering Techniques

As we navigate through the labyrinth of modern life, clutter has become an unwelcome companion. However, clutter doesn't only exist in the physical world. One often overlooked but equally significant aspect of decluttering is addressing digital clutter. In today's technology-driven society, managing digital clutter is crucial for achieving mental clarity, which plays a vital role in comprehensive decluttering efforts.

Digital clutter manifests as unnecessary emails, unorganized files, and overflowing photo galleries on our devices. This can have a profound impact on mental clarity, just as physical clutter does. Your brain responds to digital chaos similarly, resulting in stress and decreased productivity. According to research, visual distractions can overwhelm our sensory input, leading to cognitive overload (Meyer & Balasco, 2021). Simplifying your digital environment not only helps reclaim your focus but also provides a sense of accomplishment.

Tackling digital clutter requires practical strategies. Start by unsubscribing from emails you no longer read. This simple act can significantly reduce the volume of unnecessary information vying for your attention. Next, think about organizing your digital files into a structured system that mirrors your physical filing habits. Just as you might sort papers into folders based on topic, create corresponding digital folders for documents, photos, and other files. A consistent naming convention and deletion of duplicate or obsolete files can go a long way in maintaining order.

Further, consider syncing your digital and physical decluttering efforts for a more holistic experience. When you organize your home, ensure your digital spaces receive equal attention. For example, as you clean out closets, take the time to delete unused apps on your phone or backup old files onto external drives. This synchronized approach not only enhances the feeling of control over your space but also strengthens your organizational skills.

To prevent digital clutter from creeping back, establish ongoing habits. Dedicate regular intervals —perhaps weekly or monthly—to review and manage digital content. During these sessions, assess your needs and eliminate what's no longer relevant. Setting up reminders or automation tools can assist in this process, ensuring you stay committed. As you cultivate these habits, you'll find that maintaining a decluttered digital environment becomes second nature.

Preventing future digital clutter not only reinforces organizational skills but also enhances overall well-being. Decluttering shouldn't be a one-time event; instead, it should become part of a continuous lifestyle choice. By integrating digital decluttering into your routine, you foster a sustainable cycle of tidiness both online and offline.

Avoid common pitfalls like ignoring backups, which are essential for safeguarding important data, or overlooking cybersecurity measures. Keeping security top of mind protects your digital life from breaches and adds another layer of peace to your decluttering journey. Embracing digital minimalism —choosing only tools and apps that truly add value—

can further simplify and streamline your digital interactions, reducing distractions and reinforcing clarity (Barone, 2023).

Bringing It All Together

In this chapter, we've explored practical strategies for managing clutter in our homes, focusing on the "One In, One Out" rule, the "12-12-12" method, and digital decluttering techniques. Each approach offers unique benefits tailored to different aspects of our busy lives, helping transform both physical and digital spaces into havens of organization and calm. By implementing the "One In, One Out" rule, we encourage mindful consumption by ensuring new items only replace those that no longer serve us, thus fostering a balanced living environment. The "12-12-12" method provides an accessible way for busy professionals to tackle clutter through small, achievable steps that align with their schedules. Meanwhile, addressing digital clutter reinforces these efforts, promoting mental clarity and reducing stress.

As we integrate these practices into our routines, we create sustainable habits that enhance our well-being and productivity. Regular reflection on what truly adds value, combined with consistent decluttering efforts, leads to a sanctuary-like home where order reigns. This organized environment supports a peaceful mind, allowing us to better manage daily challenges. Remember, the goal is not perfection but progress—small steps taken consistently can lead to significant changes. Through conscious choices and ongoing commitment, we cultivate a lifestyle that balances demands and nurtures serenity, ultimately improving our quality of life.

Reference List

Barone, R. (2023, December 13). *A New Year's Resolution: Five Steps To Reduce Organizational Digital Clutter* . Forbes. https://www.forbes.com/councils/forbestechcouncil/2023/12/13/a-new-years-resolution-five-steps-to-reduce-organizational-digital-clutter/

Clutterfree Inspiration: Two Beautiful Transformations : zen habits . (n.d.). Zenhabits.net. https://zenhabits.net/transformations/

Ginny. (2024, January 10). *Sustainable Decluttering for an Eco-Friendly Home* . Naked Sustainability. https://nakedsustainability.com/sustainable-decluttering/

Meyer, S., & Balasco, R. (2021, June 28). *Dealing with digital clutter: What it is and 6 places to practice digital minimalism* . Thezebra.com; The Zebra. https://www.thezebra.com/resources/home/digital-clutter/

Prevent Consumption Clutter with These Mindful Shopping Habits . (n.d.). Minima. https://www.minimaonline.com/journal/prevent-consumption-clutter-with-these-mindful-shopping-habits

Watson, T. (2024, September 29). *The Life-Changing Magic of Decluttering* . Substack.com; Tom Watson's Newsletter. https://substack.com/

home/post/p-149523733?
utm_campaign=post&utm_medium=web

Chapter 7

Organizational Tools and Resources

Organizational tools and resources are essential to maintaining a tidy and functional living or working space. These tools, far from being mere accessories, serve as the backbone of an efficient decluttering process, allowing busy professionals to streamline their environments amidst hectic schedules. When life becomes a whirlwind of tasks and commitments, finding solace in order is not just helpful—it's necessary. The strategic use of organizational supplies provides that much-needed clarity and peace, transforming chaotic corners into purposeful areas. This chapter will delve into how these indispensable tools can revolutionize the way we interact with our spaces, emphasizing the importance of equipping oneself with the right resources.

Throughout this chapter, readers will explore a variety of organizational tools designed to tackle clutter head-on. From versatile bins and baskets that offer elegant solutions for categorizing belongings to innovative shelving units that maximize vertical storage, each tool plays a unique role in promoting orderliness. Additionally, the chapter will discuss the significance of filing systems in managing both physical documents and digital records, offering strategies to maintain essential paperwork without succumbing to overwhelming piles. By understanding the specific functions of each resource, readers will learn how to integrate them effectively into their daily routines, ensuring that every inch of their environment serves a purpose. As we dissect these tools and resources, the aim is to offer practical insights and guidance tailored to fit the demanding lifestyles of professionals seeking balance and organization.

Identify Essential Organizational Supplies

In today's fast-paced world, maintaining an organized living space can seem like a daunting task, especially for busy professionals who find themselves juggling myriad responsibilities. To streamline your environment and create a conducive living or working space, it is essential to understand the value of organizational supplies. The right tools not only simplify the process of decluttering but also help maintain order in the long run.

One of the most versatile and effective solutions in tackling clutter comes in the form of bins and baskets. These come in various sizes and styles, allowing for the sorting and categorization of almost anything—from seldom-used seasonal items to everyday essentials. Having dedicated containers for different categories of belongings ensures that everything has its own place. For instance, you might use larger baskets to store blankets and pillows, medium ones for toys or craft supplies, and smaller bins for office necessities such as pens and staplers. A strategic placement of these baskets around your home or office helps prevent clutter from sneaking back into your carefully curated spaces. As a guideline, label each bin or basket to designate its purpose clearly. This simple step can dramatically reduce time spent searching for items and minimize the risk of reorganizing frequently (recipes et al., 2020).

Next, shelving units serve as another indispensable resource in maximizing space efficiency. By embracing vertical storage, you free up floor space while maintaining clear visibility of stored items. Adjustable shelves are particularly beneficial as they can be tailored to accommodate items of varying heights and sizes, ensuring efficient use of available space. Consider installing shelves in underutilized areas such as corners, above doors, or even within closets to maximize potential storage. The advantage of shelving lies in its ability to display items at eye level, making them easily accessible and reducing the likelihood of items being forgotten or unused over time. When organizing your shelves, keep frequently used items within easy reach, while placing less frequently needed items higher up or further back. This not only keeps your daily routine smooth but also makes it simpler to return each item to its rightful spot after use (This Old House, 2020).

Furthermore, filing systems play a crucial role in managing documents and reducing paper clutter—a common issue in both personal and professional settings. Whether opting for traditional color-coded folders or embracing digital solutions, having a clear filing strategy aids in the swift retrieval of important documents. Physical files can be organized by category, date, or importance, using separate colors for easy identification. Meanwhile, digital filing systems offer the added benefits of accessibility and security. Cloud-based storage, for instance, not only keeps digital records accessible from anywhere but also allows for automatic updates and backups, safeguarding against data loss. It's helpful to regularly review and declutter your filing system, discarding outdated materials and ensuring all necessary documents are current and accessible. Implementing a clear naming convention in digital systems can further enhance searchability and organization.

The combination of these organizational tools fosters a more harmonious and productive living or work environment. Busy professionals, often time-starved and overwhelmed, will appreciate the ease and efficiency these resources bring to their daily lives. Bins and baskets, shelving units, and filing systems together contribute to a structured approach to dealing with clutter, transforming chaotic spaces into orderly and calm environments.

Moreover, employing these tools in conjunction creates a holistic system of organization adaptable to any lifestyle or space. They allow for personalized customization depending on individual needs and preferences, all while keeping the overarching objective of decluttering in focus. Consequently, the stress associated with disorganization diminishes, paving the way for increased productivity and peace of mind.

Utilize Technology for Inventory Management

In today's digital age, busy professionals face the challenge of maintaining an organized living space while juggling demanding work schedules. Fortunately, technology offers a range of tools that can streamline and enhance your organizing efforts, making it easier to manage clutter and maintain order. Let's explore how inventory apps, task management tools, cloud storage, and social media groups can play a crucial role in achieving this goal.

Inventory apps provide a comprehensive solution for tracking household items and their storage locations. These apps enable you to catalog your belongings with ease, often supporting barcode scanning or manual entry. By keeping a digital record of your possessions, you gain visual reminders of what you own, which helps prevent duplicate purchases and eliminates the need for unnecessary shopping trips. For example, when you're at the store and can't remember whether you already have a specific kitchen gadget, simply checking your inventory app saves time and money. This organizational strategy not only curtails impulse buying but also promotes efficient use of storage space by ensuring every item has its designated place. With features like automatic reminders for expired food items or household supplies running low, these apps take inventory management to the next level (Kholodenko, 2022).

Task management tools offer another layer of support by helping you organize decluttering projects into manageable tasks with set deadlines. These tools encourage commitment and prioritization through timely reminders and notifications. By breaking down large projects into smaller, actionable steps, you can tackle clutter more effectively, one task at a time. Whether it's clearing out a closet or organizing a garage, setting milestone goals in a task management tool keeps you motivated and focused. Moreover, these systems often allow sharing of lists or progress with family members or roommates, fostering a collaborative approach to maintaining an organized home (Kholodenko, 2022).

Cloud storage solutions are indispensable for digitally backing up important documents and ensuring they remain accessible from anywhere. In today's fast-paced world, paper clutter can quickly accumulate, leading to misplaced or lost documents. By scanning vital papers and storing them in the cloud, you create a virtual filing cabinet that is both secure and conveniently accessible. Automatic updates and organization features in cloud storage solutions help maintain order without constant manual intervention. For instance, services like Google Drive or Dropbox offer users peace of mind knowing that even if physical documents are lost or damaged, digital copies are safely archived. This approach not only reduces physical clutter but also streamlines finding and retrieving information whenever needed (*IoT in Inventory Management: The Complete Guide for 2024*, 2024).

Social media groups serve as vibrant communities where individuals can find motivation and tips for overcoming organizational challenges. By connecting with others facing similar struggles, you gain access to a wealth of knowledge and experiences shared by many. Joining online groups dedicated to decluttering or minimalism provides encouragement as members share before-and-after photos of their transformed spaces, inspiring others to do the same. Additionally, these communities foster accountability, as participants can post their own goals and progress, receiving feedback and encouragement from peers. Such interactions create a sense of belonging and reinforce ongoing efforts to maintain a tidy environment.

For those new to these technologies, it may be helpful to follow some general guidelines to maximize their effectiveness. When choosing an inventory app, ensure it caters to your specific needs, such as allowing custom categories or alert settings. Begin with a small section of your home to gradually build your digital inventory without feeling overwhelmed. With task management tools, prioritize tasks based on urgency and importance. Remember to celebrate completed tasks, acknowledging your progress. For cloud storage, start by digitizing essential documents while creating a logical folder structure for easy retrieval. Regularly back up new documents and keep your storage sorted and updated.

Explore Storage Solutions for Small Spaces

In today's fast-paced world, maximizing space is more crucial than ever, especially for busy professionals who find it challenging to maintain an organized living area. The key lies in utilizing clever storage solutions that fit seamlessly into one's lifestyle. Here, we explore practical and efficient storage options tailored for individuals dealing with space constraints, ensuring that every inch serves a purpose without compromising on style or functionality.

Under-bed storage is a highly effective solution for managing limited space. By introducing bed risers, one can significantly increase the storage capacity beneath the bed. This approach is perfect for storing seasonal or seldom-used items such as winter coats, extra bedding, or holiday decorations, keeping them out of sight yet easily accessible. Utilizing this often-overlooked space not only declutters the living area but also keeps belongings organized and within reach when needed (2016).

Next, consider wall-mounted shelves, which are ideal for freeing up floor space and adding aesthetic value. Floating shelves, in particular, present a modern look while offering storage opportunities. They can be strategically placed to suit various heights and needs, holding anything from books and decorative pieces to kitchen essentials. This flexibility allows for personalization, making it easier to create a visually pleasing environment that reflects one's taste. Moreover, the vertical arrangement ensures that no space goes unused, transforming walls into functional and attractive storage zones.

Multi-functional furniture is another innovative way to optimize small spaces. Furniture like storage ottomans and Murphy beds serve dual purposes, catering to both utility and space conservation. Storage ottomans offer hidden compartments for stowing away blankets or magazines, while Murphy beds fold away when not in use, opening up valuable floor space during the day. These versatile pieces allow rooms to adapt to different functions, all while maintaining a tidy appearance. For instance, a living room can quickly become a guest bedroom without sacrificing order or comfort.

Hooks and pegboards present a fantastic solution for organizing tools and accessories by taking advantage of vertical wall space. Whether in a garage, kitchen, or office, these systems keep frequently used items within easy reach and help personalize one's decor. Pegboards, in particular, can be customized with various hooks and attachments to accommodate diverse storage needs, from hanging utensils to organizing crafting supplies (*Amazon.com*, 2014). Not only do they maximize storage efficiency, but they also add a unique flair to any room, balancing functionality with personal style.

Each of these solutions offers distinct advantages that cater to the needs of those navigating compact living areas. Implementing under-bed storage, for instance, addresses the challenge of storing bulky, seasonal items without cluttering prime living space. Bed risers create a discreet and effective storage area, allowing for a cleaner, more organized home. In comparison, wall-mounted shelves provide a stylish way to display and store belongings, enhancing the room's decor while effectively utilizing vertical space. Their adaptability means they can be adjusted to suit changing needs or preferences over time, ensuring they remain a relevant addition to any home.

Similarly, multi-functional furniture introduces an element of adaptability that is particularly beneficial for those with dynamic lifestyles. Busy professionals can appreciate the seamless transition between different room functions—transforming a communal area into a private retreat with ease and elegance. Such furniture optimizes spatial arrangements without compromising on comfort or utility, perfectly aligning with modern-day demands for efficiency and simplicity.

Lastly, utilizing hooks and pegboards encourages thoughtful organization of smaller items and tools while providing a creative outlet for personalization. Their versatility makes them suitable for almost any setting, from kitchens to workshops, promoting orderliness without losing sight of individual expression. They leverage otherwise unused wall space, converting potential into practical and appealing storage solutions.

Concluding Thoughts

In this chapter, we've delved into the array of tools and resources available to help busy professionals manage and streamline their living spaces. We've explored practical items like bins and baskets for categorizing belongings, efficient shelving units for maximizing vertical space, and filing systems for organizing important documents. These essential organizational supplies not only simplify the process of decluttering but also help maintain long-term order, ensuring that each item in your home or office has a designated place. By strategically utilizing these resources, you can create an environment that fosters productivity and reduces stress.

Moreover, we've highlighted the role of technology in modern inventory management, emphasizing how digital solutions can enhance organizational efforts. Inventory apps, task management tools, cloud storage, and supportive online communities serve as valuable allies in keeping chaos at bay. With these technologies, you can track belongings, manage tasks, secure important documents, and find encouragement from others on similar journeys toward minimalism. Together, these organizational strategies offer a comprehensive approach to managing clutter, empowering you to transform your space into one that reflects both efficiency and tranquility.

Reference List

(2016). Thechaosninja.com. https:// www.thechaosninja.com/post/maximizing-small-spaces-clever-storage-solutions-for-tiny-homes

Amazon.com . (2014). Amazon.com. https://www.amazon.com/Pegboard-Floating-Organizer-Bathroom-Entryway/dp/B09ZYV5CZN

IoT in Inventory Management: The Complete Guide for 2024 . (2024, October 4). Imaginovation | Top Web & Mobile App Development Company Raleigh. https://imaginovation.net/blog/iot-in-inventory-management/

Kholodenko, O. (2022, August 26). *Technology in Inventory Management – Technological Warehousing* . CodeIT. https://codeit.us/blog/technologies-in-inventory-management

This Old House. (2020, January 19). *A Comprehensive Guide to Storage & Organization* . This Old House. https://www.thisoldhouse.com/storage-organization/21072567/all-about-storage-organization recipes, K. sharing, Ideas, T. N. C., Decorating, P. for P. as W. as, & Pinterest, creating D. projects for her home F. T. I. (2020, May 29). *42 Essential Organizing Products For Your Home* . Clutter Keeper®. https://www.clutterkeeper.com/essential-organizing-products-for-your-home/

Chapter 8

Maintaining a Clutter-Free Home

Maintaining a clutter-free home requires the establishment of regular habits that align with your daily life. With demanding work schedules, it's easy to let organization slide, leading to a chaotic living environment. Yet, preventing this chaos and fostering a sense of calm and orderliness at home is possible, even for the busiest professionals. The key lies in embedding small, consistent actions into your routine, transforming tidying up from an overwhelming task into a manageable, refreshing practice. A well-organized home not only enhances your physical environment but also contributes significantly to your mental well-being, allowing you to tackle each day with clarity and peace of mind.

In this chapter, we delve into practical strategies designed to help busy individuals maintain a neat and organized living space. We explore the role of family involvement and how shared responsibilities can make upkeep more efficient and less burdensome. Learn about setting specific times for decluttering that fit seamlessly into your current schedule, ensuring tasks don't become overwhelming. We will discuss methods to integrate organizational practices naturally into your daily routines without creating additional stress. Additionally, we'll address the importance of reflecting on these routines to continually improve and adapt them to suit changing circumstances within your household. Each section provides a step-by-step guide to developing a clutter-free lifestyle that enhances both personal tranquility and family harmony.

Develop Daily Tidy-Up Routines

Maintaining a clutter-free home may seem like a daunting task, especially for busy professionals who juggle demanding schedules. However, by fostering sustainable habits, tidying up can become a manageable and even enjoyable part of your daily routine. The journey to an organized home begins with encouraging family participation, designating specific times for decluttering, integrating cleaning into existing routines, and reflecting on the success of these efforts.

Encouraging family participation is essential in promoting teamwork and shared responsibility. An orderly home should not be the responsibility of one person; rather, it is a collaborative effort that involves every member of the household. By allocating chores based on skills and interests, families can make tasks more engaging and less burdensome. For instance, someone who enjoys gardening could take on plant care, while another who prefers culinary activities might handle kitchen duties (Stephanie, 2024). This approach ensures that tasks are completed effectively and enjoyably, transforming chores into opportunities for skill development and cooperation.

Creating a fair system for rotating duties is also beneficial. Rotating chores prevents any individual from being stuck permanently with undesirable tasks, thus maintaining harmony within the household. This method not only fosters a sense of fairness and shared responsibility but also broadens everyone's skill set as they tackle different tasks over time (Stephanie, 2024). Therefore, involving everyone in the process can simplify the path to a tidy home by distributing the workload evenly and cultivating a spirit of collaboration.

The next step in creating sustainable tidying habits is to designate specific daily time slots for efficient decluttering efforts. Managing time efficiently transforms overwhelming tasks into smaller, manageable ones. By setting aside just 15 to 30 minutes each day, you can address various clutter hotspots without feeling overwhelmed (CoCo, 2024). Consider implementing time-blocking techniques, where specific periods are allocated for certain tasks. For example, establishing a quick evening decluttering session can help keep messes from accumulating overnight. According to Cal Newport's "Deep Work," this focused approach enhances productivity and helps maintain balance between work and personal life (Stephanie, 2024).

Incorporating tidying into existing routines further streamlines the process. By weaving cleaning tasks into established daily rituals, such as meal prep or bedtime, tidying can become second nature. For instance, making unloading the dishwasher part of your morning routine can maximize efficiency, while loading it at night ensures that everything is in order by the next day (CoCo, 2024). Similarly, wiping down kitchen counters after meals or sorting mail upon its arrival can prevent clutter from piling up.

This integration makes tidying feel less like a chore and more like a natural extension of everyday activities, saving both time and energy.

Moreover, technology can be leveraged to track tasks and ensure consistent follow-through. Various apps and tools are available to help organize tasks, send reminders, and map out cleaning schedules. These digital aids act as supportive companions in maintaining a clutter-free environment, ensuring nothing falls through the cracks amidst hectic workdays. By utilizing these technological solutions, busy professionals can streamline their organizational efforts without sacrificing precious time.

Reflecting on the success of these newly formed habits is crucial in reinforcing positive behavior. Taking a moment to recognize the achievements and benefits of maintaining a tidy home can be motivating and energizing. Regular reflection sessions allow you to evaluate what strategies are working well and identify areas for improvement. Celebrating small victories, such as completing a week of successful tidying, builds momentum and encourages continued commitment to these routines (Stephanie, 2024). Additionally, acknowledging the positive impact on stress levels and overall well-being reinforces the value of maintaining these habits, turning them into lifelong practices.

Reflection also serves as a tool for adaptability. Family needs and schedules change over time, and so should your approach to home organization. What worked a month ago might require adjustment today. By consistently reviewing the effectiveness of implemented strategies, you can adapt cleaning routines to fit evolving circumstances. Engaging in open communication with household members about these reflections ensures that everyone is on the same page and contributes to the collective effort toward a clutter-free home.

Set Rules for New Purchases

Maintaining a clutter-free home can be a challenging yet rewarding endeavor. The key is to establish habits that not only keep your living space organized but also ensure mindful consumption, preventing clutter from sneaking back into your life. This subpoint offers practical guidelines designed to support busy professionals like you in maintaining a tidy environment without adding stress to your already demanding schedule.

One effective strategy is the 'One In, One Out' policy, which serves as a simple rule for keeping balance in your home organization efforts. Each time a new item enters your home, an existing item should make its way out. This practice encourages you to critically assess new purchases against the backdrop of what you already own. Removing older or less useful items helps maintain a harmonious balance in your household, freeing space and reducing unnecessary accumulation (Houlton, 2024). Implementing this policy doesn't just declutter; it prompts you to reflect on what truly adds value or joy to your life, aligning with Marie Kondo's celebrated principle (Godreau, 2024).

Another crucial aspect of maintaining a clutter-free home involves identifying essential purchases. It's easy to fall prey to consumerism, especially amidst busy schedules where convenience often takes precedence over necessity. Before making a purchase, consider how much joy or utility the item will bring into your life. Ask yourself if it's something you'll truly benefit from or merely a fleeting want. Making intentional choices ensures that every addition complements your lifestyle rather than clutters it. While the one-in, one-out concept directly ties to physical belongings, the idea of mindful consumption translates to various aspects of life, encouraging careful consideration of digital and emotional spaces too.

Limiting impulse buying can significantly contribute to a cleaner and more organized home. To curb impulsive decisions, introduce a waiting period before purchasing non-essential items. Consider implementing a 48-hour rule: if you feel inclined to buy something on a whim, wait two days and reassess its importance in your life. Often, this pause allows you to evaluate whether the item is a true necessity or simply a passing desire. Such practices foster financial prudence and help prioritize meaningful acquisitions over short-lived gratifications (Houlton, 2024).

Educating others in your household about these principles can create a supportive and cohesive environment. Sharing the philosophy behind mindful purchasing and decluttering practices can influence collective behavior, making it easier to maintain a clutter-free space collaboratively. Encourage family members or roommates to embrace similar practices, fostering discussions around why specific habits are beneficial. When everyone is on board, a communal effort toward maintaining an organized home becomes more attainable and less burdensome for any single individual.

In a hectic world, integrating these habits into daily routines requires strategic planning and open communication. Start small by involving others in implementing the one-in, one-out rule during joint household purchases. Discuss the importance of identifying what's truly valuable to each member of the household, allowing personal preferences and necessities to guide purchasing decisions collectively. It's also essential to regularly review these strategies to ensure they remain practical and beneficial for everyone involved.

Finally, these approaches highlight the broader impact of clutter on mental health and well-being. A cluttered home can contribute to feelings of chaos and overwhelm, while a clean, organized environment fosters relaxation and focus. By adopting these habits, you're not only creating a functional living space but also enhancing your mental clarity and peace of mind. With fewer distractions, there's more room for creativity and productivity, essential components for thriving in both personal and professional spheres (Godreau, 2024).

Conduct Regular Decluttering Check-Ins

In the bustling lives of busy professionals, maintaining a clutter-free home can often feel like an unattainable dream. However, with the right strategies in place, it is more than achievable—it is transformative. A critical strategy to ensure this transformation is the consistent evaluation of living spaces to maintain tidiness and address any accumulating clutter. This proactive approach not only helps in managing existing clutter but also in preventing future chaos.

The first step towards achieving this goal is setting monthly calendar reminders for regular organization check-ins. These check-ins are crucial because they prompt you to pause amidst your busy schedule and dedicate time to assess your surroundings. By treating these sessions as essential appointments rather than optional tasks, you prioritize them just as you would a work meeting or a social obligation. These reminders act as gentle nudges, ensuring that no matter how hectic life gets, you have designated times to tackle clutter head-on.

During these organization check-ins, specific attention should be given to high-traffic areas.

Spaces such as the kitchen, living room, and entryways are prone to becoming cluttered due to frequent use. Regular evaluations of these areas help maintain ease of use and comfort. For instance, ensuring that pathways are clear not only enhances the aesthetic appeal but also improves safety by minimizing tripping hazards. Additionally, keeping items in their proper places makes daily routines smoother, allowing for quick access to essentials and reducing stress levels.

Reflection plays a pivotal role during these check-in sessions, as it encourages a deeper understanding of your organizational habits. By taking a moment to reflect on what strategies have worked or failed, you can continuously improve your approach to decluttering. This reflection also serves as an avenue for better communication within the household. Discussing the current state of the home and sharing insights can lead to more effective collaboration among family members. It can even open up opportunities for brainstorming new ideas to tackle persistent clutter issues.

Furthermore, adapting strategies based on household feedback is essential for meeting evolving needs. Just as businesses adapt to changing market conditions, households too must be flexible in their approaches to tidiness. Feedback can illuminate areas where traditional methods fall short and highlight unique challenges faced by individual family members. By incorporating this feedback into your organizational strategies, you create a dynamic system that grows alongside your household.

Implementing individual responsibilities can significantly enhance the effectiveness of these efforts. Assigning specific tasks or areas to each family member not only distributes the workload evenly but also fosters a sense of ownership. When individuals take responsibility for certain spaces, they are more likely to maintain them consistently, knowing that others rely on them. This approach not only reinforces accountability but also strengthens teamwork within the household.

To support these initiatives, creating simple guidelines can be beneficial. For instance, establishing a guideline for systematic evaluations ensures that everyone knows what to expect during check-ins. Clear parameters on what constitutes clutter, which areas need priority, and how to evaluate success can streamline the process, making it easier for everyone involved.

Wrapping Up

Throughout this chapter, we've explored effective strategies to establish habits for maintaining an organized home. By involving every member of the household in daily tidy-up routines, the burden of chores is lightened, and a sense of shared responsibility is fostered. Encouraging teamwork through rotating duties not only prevents monotony but also expands everyone's skillset. Setting aside specific times for decluttering helps manage tasks efficiently, turning them into manageable parts of your day. Integrating these routines into existing habits makes tidying up seem less like a chore and more like a seamless part of everyday life. Moreover, utilizing technology to keep track of tasks can provide busy professionals with the structure needed to maintain their homes in order.

Emphasizing reflection on these practices reinforces positive behavior, allowing you to celebrate successes and adjust strategies as needed. Regularly evaluating what works ensures that habits remain effective as family needs evolve over time. Establishing guidelines for mindful consumption is another important aspect discussed, where methods like the 'One In, One Out' rule help maintain balance by prompting consideration before making new purchases. Limiting impulse buying further supports a clutter-free environment while educating household members fosters collective efforts towards organization. Ultimately, the transformation achieved by integrating these habits goes beyond a clean space—it enhances mental well-being by reducing stress and fostering relaxation, providing a foundation for a productive personal and professional life.

Reference List

11 Benefits of a Clean Work Space for Superior productivity . (n.d.). Www.sterlingcleaningnyc.com. https://www.sterlingcleaningnyc.com/blog/ benefits-of-clean-work-space

Birt, J. (2022, September 30). *11 Benefits of Maintaining a Clean and Orderly Workplace* . Indeed Career Guide. https://www.indeed.com/ career-advice/career-development/benefits-of-functionality-in-the-workplace

CoCo. (2024, January 22). *Modern Day Cleaning Schedule Made Easy* . Thecrownedgoat.com. https://thecrownedgoat.com/modern-day-cleaning-schedule-made-easy/

Godreau, J. (2024, March 22). *Declutter Your Home, Declutter Your Mind: The Path to Mental Clarity* . Mindful Health Solutions. https://mindfulhealthsolutions.com/declutter-your-home-declutter-your-mind-the-path-to-mental-clarity/

Houlton, L. (2024, January 25). *Is the "one-in, one-out" rule the only decluttering technique you'll ever need?* Homesandgardens.com; Homes & Gardens. https://www.homesandgardens.com/solved/one-in-one-out-rule

Stephanie. (2024, April 21). *Mastering Home Management: Essential Tips for Busy Families - Hello,Nanny!* Hello,Nanny! https://hellonanny.com/home-management-tips/

Chapter 9

Tackling Emotional Attachments

Tackling emotional attachments is an integral part of the decluttering process for busy professionals. Our possessions often hold more than just practical or decorative value; they are deeply intertwined with our emotions and memories. These sentimental ties can present unique challenges in maintaining a tidy living space, especially for those with demanding schedules. By understanding the psychological aspects of attachment, individuals can begin to navigate these emotional barriers with greater ease. The complexity lies not only in the physical act of decluttering but also in recognizing the emotions that bind us to certain items, making it difficult to let go even when their utility has waned.

This chapter delves into the reasons behind our emotional connections to objects and explores how these attachments influence our ability to declutter effectively. It examines the role of nostalgia, guilt, and psychological ownership in shaping our decisions around what to keep and what to discard. By shedding light on these emotional dynamics, the chapter provides insights and strategies to help readers make informed choices about their belongings. Whether it's holding onto family heirlooms or gifts from loved ones, this exploration offers practical advice for evaluating sentimental items thoughtfully. Readers will learn how to separate the object from the memory it represents, allowing them to honor their past without being overwhelmed by clutter in the present.

Understand the Psychology of Attachment

In the journey of decluttering, understanding the influence of emotional connections with items can provide clarity and solutions for those seeking to organize their living spaces. Our attachment to objects often goes beyond mere aesthetics or utility; it delves into the realm of sentiment where emotions like happiness, sadness, guilt, and nostalgia intertwine with our belongings.

Sentimental value plays a pivotal role in how we perceive and ultimately manage our possessions. Items such as family heirlooms or gifts from loved ones carry emotional weight that transcends their physical form. For many busy professionals, these objects act as time capsules, evoking memories of significant life events and treasured relationships. This emotional complexity can make decision-making around decluttering challenging. When an object sparks joy or sadness, it can cloud judgment and hinder the ability to part with it, even when it's no longer practical to keep.

The impact of nostalgia further complicates the process. Nostalgia is a powerful emotion that binds us to the past, often infusing everyday objects with a sense of continuity and identity. These sentimental ties can be comforting yet misleading. Recognizing the triggers of nostalgia can help individuals separate their emotions from the items they hold dear. For instance, an old book might remind someone of peaceful childhood afternoons spent reading, making it difficult to let go. By acknowledging that the memory lives within them rather than the object, individuals may find it easier to declutter without feeling a sense of loss.

Feelings of shame and guilt frequently surface during decluttering endeavors. Many people experience guilt about discarding gifts or inherited items due to perceived obligations towards those who bestowed them. This emotional burden can block the path to a more organized environment. Understanding that personal values should guide decisions rather than societal expectations is crucial. Embracing one's priorities can alleviate these feelings, allowing for a more guilt-free approach to decluttering. Accepting that honoring the intent behind a gift doesn't necessarily mean keeping it forever can foster a healthier relationship with belongings.

The concept of psychological ownership also influences attachment levels. The longer we possess something, the more attached we become, sometimes to the point where the item feels like an extension of ourselves. This illusion can create resistance to letting go, rooted in the belief that parting with an item means losing a piece of our identity. Identifying this cognitive bias can empower individuals to make conscious choices about their possessions. Realizing that who we are isn't defined by what we own is liberating and can facilitate the decluttering process.

Emotional attachments to possessions can be seen not merely as obstacles but as opportunities for introspection and growth. They invite individuals to explore what truly holds value in their lives and to appreciate the memories associated with these items without being weighed down by their physical presence. By examining the narratives and emotions tied to their belongings, individuals can cultivate a deeper understanding of themselves and their past.

Taking steps to address these emotional barriers can transform the decluttering experience from a daunting task into a mindful practice. Busy professionals, whose schedules often leave little room for reflection, might benefit from setting aside dedicated time to consider the emotional stories their possessions tell. This intentional pause can lead to more informed and meaningful decluttering decisions.

Ultimately, recognizing the interplay between emotional connections and decluttering equips individuals with the awareness needed to manage their living spaces effectively. Whether it's choosing to keep a few cherished items or liberating oneself from unnecessary clutter, these insights open the door to a balanced environment where emotional well-being and practicality coexist. With a better understanding of how emotions influence decluttering, individuals can embark on this journey with confidence, paving the way for more organized and fulfilling lives.

Citations:
(juliec, 2024)

Establish Criteria for Keeping Sentimental Items

Understanding which sentimental items to keep can be challenging, especially for busy professionals who find it difficult to maintain an organized living space. To address this, a structured approach is essential. The focus should initially be on prioritizing quality over quantity. This means taking stock of the items you own and evaluating each for its importance in your life. In doing so, remember that fewer meaningful items often carry greater emotional weight than an overwhelming collection. By concentrating on what truly resonates with you, you create a curated collection that enhances your living environment rather than complicates it.

Think about the memories associated with these items. Instead of clinging to every physical object connected to a cherished moment, concentrate on creating rituals or stories that celebrate those memories. For instance, instead of keeping all of your childhood toys, consider selecting one or two that represent the happiest moments, and then share stories about them with friends or family members during gatherings. This not only enshrines the memory but also keeps it alive in a more interactive way. These practices transform experiences into living narratives, allowing memories to remain significant without physical clutter.

Functional value is another critical aspect to consider when deciding what to keep. Each item should serve a practical purpose in your life, either by being useful or bringing joy whenever used or seen. For busy professionals, merging utility with sentiment can streamline your surroundings while retaining personal significance. For example, a beautiful bowl gifted by a loved one can be displayed prominently if it holds keys or change, serving both a functional purpose and emotional connection. Regularly using such items maintains their purpose in your life, thereby justifying their presence.

To ensure the sentimental value of items remains clear and relevant, it's essential to reassess your collection periodically. As life evolves, so do your emotional attachments and priorities. Establishing a schedule for revisiting your items provides the opportunity to reflect on what still holds meaning and what may have served its purpose. A bi-annual review could coincide with seasonal changes or personal milestones, offering a moment to decide whether the emotional attachment to certain items has diminished. Through regular assessment, you cultivate a conscious relationship with your belongings, reinforcing their place in your life or allowing space for new memories.

Establishing guidelines around these ideas helps achieve clarity and focus, making the decision-making process less daunting. With the emphasis on quality over quantity, explore a simple rule like the 'one-in, one-out' policy to manage your sentimental inventory actively. Every new addition could mean saying goodbye to an old one, ensuring that only the most treasured items are part of your curated collection.

Creating memory rituals doesn't have to be complex. Commit to telling a favorite anecdote behind a cherished item at least once every gathering when family or friends visit. This practice enriches your interactions and reinforces the item's emotional significance without accumulating additional physical objects.

Assessing functional value operates well with categorization. Divide your belongings into 'must-have' and 'nice-to-have' categories. Must-have items should provide clear utility or profound joy. If an item doesn't fall into either category, question its place in your home. This framework guides you in aligning your possessions with your lifestyle, ensuring they aid rather than hinder your daily routine.

Revisiting items regularly accommodates changing values and needs. Set reminders on your calendar to engage in reflection exercises, asking questions like: Does this item still spark joy? Is there a fresh story or new context that increases its relevance now? Taking the time to answer these queries grants insight into your shifting priorities, supporting ongoing decluttering efforts.

Practice Letting Go with Minimal Regret

When decluttering sentimental items, it's essential to cultivate a mindset that reduces regret. Visualizing loss is a powerful first step. Imagine your space without certain items, and consider how you feel.

This visualization helps distinguish between what truly holds importance and what has merely occupied space over time. For instance, imagine a living room free from cluttered shelves or a bedroom that feels more like a sanctuary than a storage unit. This exercise clarifies which objects serve a meaningful purpose versus those that have blended into the background without significant emotional attachment.

Temporary removal can be an effective strategy for processing emotions tied to belongings. Consider this a trial period where items are placed in a box and stored out of sight. During this time, pay attention to your emotional responses. Do you miss the items? Do they come to mind unprompted? You may realize that absence does make the heart grow fonder for some things, while for others, it brings relief and clarity. This approach allows you to process any underlying emotional connections before making permanent decisions, offering a buffer zone to deal with potential regret proactively.

Creating a 'goodbye' ritual offers a meaningful way to let go of items. These rituals can provide closure, helping to honor and release possessions gracefully. They can be as simple as saying a few words of thanks, creating a small ceremony, or writing a note about what the item meant to you and the new space you're making for growth. By engaging in such practices, you're providing yourself with a tangible method to acknowledge the significance of these items, thus easing the emotional transition involved in letting go. It transforms decluttering from a mere physical task into a mindful act of personal reflection and appreciation.

Transitioning from a mindset of regret to one of opportunity is crucial in reframing your perspective on decluttering. Instead of focusing on the perceived loss, turn your attention to the benefits of having a more organized and intentional living space. Decluttering can lead to newfound opportunities, such as experiencing peace, creativity, and even financial gain by selling or donating items. Embrace the idea that letting go makes space not just physically but also emotionally and mentally, allowing for new experiences and memories to take root in your life.

Consider how different life priorities might be better supported by a decluttered space; a home office that's no longer overcrowded can become a haven of productivity, or a cleared kitchen counter can inspire new culinary adventures. These benefits reinforce the positive aspects of decluttering, focusing not on what's lost but on what's gained—whether that's a clearer living environment, mental clarity, or simply the joy of knowing you've passed cherished items onto someone who will value them.

As you work through these steps, remember that change in mindset requires patience and practice. It's normal to feel resistance when parting with sentimental items, yet each step taken towards releasing these attachments is a step toward embracing simplicity and tranquility in your surroundings. Practically speaking, begin with areas less emotionally charged, and gradually work up to more challenging items, thereby building confidence in your ability to discern true necessity and sentimentality.

Moreover, practical guidelines such as tackling one area at a time prevent overwhelming feelings and ensure focus remains sharp. A focused approach avoids hasty decisions or the inadvertent retention of items out of sheer exhaustion. Additionally, maintaining a decluttered space is easier once the initial emotional hurdles are overcome, turning meticulous upkeep into a rewarding practice rather than a repetitive chore.

While the emotional journey of letting go varies for each person, recognizing and employing strategies like visualizing loss, temporary removal, goodbye rituals, and reframing regret help facilitate a smoother transition. These strategies serve as tools that not only address the physical act of sorting and discarding but also tend to the emotional layers interwoven with possessions. It's important to personalize them to fit individual routines and lifestyles, ensuring the process is sustainable long-term, especially for busy professionals seeking quick, efficient solutions that seamlessly integrate into their packed schedules.

Final Insights

This chapter has explored the emotional complexities of decluttering, particularly when it comes to sentimental items that hold memories and emotions. Understanding our attachment to these belongings is crucial in managing living spaces effectively. Items like family heirlooms or gifts often carry deep emotional significance, which can cloud decision-making. Acknowledging these feelings rather than ignoring them allows individuals to approach decluttering with empathy toward themselves. By recognizing the triggers of nostalgia, guilt, and psychological ownership, individuals can distinguish between their emotions and possessions, ultimately making more conscious choices about what to keep.

As busy professionals striving for a balanced life, incorporating thoughtful strategies can transform decluttering from a chore into a mindful practice. Regularly revisiting and reassessing cherished belongings ensures they remain relevant to one's current life stage and priorities. Engaging in memory rituals and maintaining only those items that genuinely bring joy or serve a purpose can lighten the emotional burden of letting go. These insights empower individuals to create a living environment that reflects both their emotional well-being and practicality, enabling them to lead more organized and fulfilling lives.

Reference List

Joshua Fields Millburn. (2015, December 14). *The Minimalists...* The Minimalists; The Minimalists. https://www.theminimalists.com/podcast/

Kings, C. A., Moulding, R., & Knight, T. (2017, July). *You are what you own: Reviewing the link between possessions, emotional attachment, and the self-concept in hoarding disorder* . Journal of Obsessive-Compulsive and Related Disorders. https://doi.org/10.1016/j.jocrd.2017.05.005

The Psychology Of Letting Go - Beyond Healing Counseling Now In 2024 . (2024, November 15). Beyond Healing Counseling. https://beyondhealingcounseling.com/the-psychology-of-letting-go/

juliec. (2024, May 16). *The Psychology of Sentimental Clutter: Letting Go of Emotional Baggage* . Professional Organiser Melbourne - Space and Time. https://spaceandtime.com.au/the-psychology-of-sentimental-clutter-letting-go-of-emotional-baggage/

Chapter 10

Adapting Strategies Over Time

Adapting strategies over time is paramount for maintaining balance in one's life, especially for busy professionals. As life's circumstances inevitably shift, so too must the methods we employ to manage our surroundings effectively. Recognizing the importance of flexibility in personal organization can lead to more harmonious living spaces that accommodate evolving needs. Whether it's a change in living arrangements, a new job, or an adjustment in family dynamics, each transition provides an opportunity to rethink and refine decluttering approaches. By embracing this concept, individuals can create environments that not only function efficiently but also contribute positively to their overall well-being.

This chapter delves into various aspects of adapting decluttering strategies as circumstances change.

Readers will explore how significant life events—such as moving, career shifts, or family additions—can necessitate reevaluating organizational methods. Seasonal adjustments and emotional influences are also discussed as factors affecting how one manages possessions. Moreover, trial and error is highlighted as a valuable tool for discovering personalized solutions that resonate with distinct lifestyles. The narrative encourages readers to view decluttering as a dynamic process, fostering continuous improvement through regular assessment and modification of strategies. By understanding and implementing adaptable techniques, busy professionals can achieve a clutter-free space that aligns with their current lifestyle demands.

Recognize the Need for Flexibility in Your Approach

Adapting to change is a vital skill in the pursuit of an organized and clutter-free home. It's not just about removing items but evolving your methods as life circumstances shift. Whether you're moving, switching jobs, or experiencing other significant changes, these events require reevaluating your approach to decluttering.

Changing Life Circumstances

Life never stays still, and neither should our decluttering strategies. Suppose you've recently moved to a new city for a job opportunity; your belongings might need to be reduced due to smaller living arrangements or a different climate. For example, if you're relocating from a rural area with ample storage space to an urban apartment, you may find that your collection of outdoor gear needs to be trimmed down. Events like marriage, having children, or even retirement can also drastically alter the way you live, thereby influencing how you manage your possessions. Each shift presents an opportunity (Iran et al., 2024) to reassess what you own, the space you occupy, and the systems you have in place to keep everything orderly.

Seasonal Adjustments

Seasons change, and so do our needs. Winter coats make sense during the colder months, but come summer, they only take up valuable space. Implementing a seasonal decluttering routine allows you to rotate items based on current requirements and available space, ensuring that your living areas are not overwhelmed. Transitioning wardrobes, storing away seasonal decor, and swapping out sports equipment can become a cathartic ritual as you prepare for the year ahead. To make this process easier, it could help to establish a routine or schedule reminders in your calendar to revisit different aspects of your home each season. Creating guidelines to remind yourself of when to perform these tasks can prevent unnecessary accumulation over time.

Emotional Response

Often overlooked, emotions have a profound impact on how we manage our things. Our emotional state can either motivate us to clear away clutter or hold us back from letting go. During stressful times, people sometimes accumulate items for comfort; conversely, periods of newfound serenity might prompt a desire to embrace minimalism and declutter. If you've ever found yourself holding onto items because they evoke strong memories or because parting with them feels like losing a piece of yourself, you are not alone. Recognizing these emotional connections allows you to address them mindfully. By acknowledging how these feelings influence your decluttering efforts, you can gently work through what's truly necessary to keep versus what you're emotionally attached to without contributing positively to your life or environment.

Trial and Error

Every home and individual is unique, making a one-size-fits-all decluttering approach impractical. Trial and error, therefore, becomes a valuable tool. Experiment with various decluttering methods until you find the ones that suit your lifestyle and personality. Some practices might resonate more than others. Methods such as the KonMari Technique, which encourages evaluating objects for joy, or the One-In-One-Out rule, where you remove an item for every new purchase, could be starting points. The idea is to be open to trying different strategies until a comfortable balance is achieved. Keeping a journal or notes of what techniques worked and what didn't can aid in refining your approach over time. This iterative process requires patience but eventually leads to a more personalized and effective system (Tanner, 2017).

Evaluate Changing Lifestyle Needs

In today's fast-paced world, adapting decluttering strategies to fit evolving personal circumstances is crucial for maintaining order and peace in one's living environment. One significant aspect to consider is family dynamics. Changes such as the addition of a new family member or children growing up can drastically affect how space is utilized. For instance, welcoming a baby requires additional storage for items like toys and clothing, which may lead to re-evaluating existing organizational systems. Conversely, when children leave for college or move out, it may be an opportune time to reassess what possessions are truly needed, thus reducing unnecessary clutter.

Similarly, a shifting work-life balance plays a pivotal role in managing clutter. As professionals juggle demanding careers, the challenge lies in balancing work commitments with home management. A job that demands long hours might mean less time available for regular tidying or sorting through belongings. To combat this, establishing simple routines or dedicating small chunks of time each week for organization can help. For busy individuals, streamlining the process by focusing on one room or section at a time rather than tackling the entire home at once can be a more manageable approach.

Health and well-being are also critical factors to contemplate. Fluctuations in physical or mental health can dramatically impact one's ability to manage household clutter. For example, a bout of illness may limit energy levels, making the idea of intense organizing daunting. In such situations, it's beneficial to prioritize comfort and only tackle essential tasks. Simple adjustments like ensuring commonly used items are within easy reach can make day-to-day life smoother without overexerting oneself.

Financial changes are yet another influential element when considering decluttering strategies. Shifts in income or financial priorities necessitate a reevaluation of how possessions are viewed and retained. A tighter budget might require letting go of luxury items or clothes that are seldom worn, while a more comfortable financial situation could lead to acquiring higher-quality but fewer items to reduce clutter. Understanding the financial value and practicality of possessions in light of current circumstances allows for informed decisions that prevent unnecessary accumulation.

To assist busy professionals in navigating these challenges, a few guidelines can be particularly helpful. First, remember that simplicity is key; focus on gradual progress rather than overnight transformations. It's about developing a system that aligns with your current lifestyle, not forcing a method that feels cumbersome or unsustainable. Secondly, involve family members in the decluttering process where possible. Shared responsibility not only distributes the workload but also encourages collective commitment to maintaining a clutter-free environment. Lastly, take advantage of technology. Digital tools and apps designed for organization can simplify management and track decluttering milestones, serving as reminders and providing motivation.

Overall, the essence of successful decluttering strategies lies in their adaptability. Life's unpredictable nature means that the decluttering approach must evolve alongside personal circumstances. Regularly assessing and adjusting strategies ensures that they remain relevant and effective in fostering an organized, serene home conducive to both personal well-being and family harmony. Recognizing that perfection isn't the goal but rather creating a space that supports your lifestyle and aspirations will lead to a more balanced, fulfilling living environment.

Update Goals and Strategies Yearly

Adapting your decluttering strategies over time is necessary to maintain an organized living space, particularly for busy professionals. The dynamic nature of life demands that we reassess and readjust our approaches to organization regularly. One effective way to ensure that your environment remains harmonious with the changes in your life is through systematic annual reviews of your organization systems.

An annual review of your home organization systems serves as a vital checkpoint to evaluate what's working and what isn't. At least once a year, take time to scrutinize each area of your living space. Assess whether the storage solutions and organizational methods currently in use are effectively meeting your needs. Are there areas consistently cluttered despite efforts to tidy them up? Acknowledging these trouble spots can provide insights into required improvements.

For busy professionals, setting aside time might seem daunting given a hectic schedule, but consider it an investment in efficiency and peace of mind. Start small by tackling one room or section at a time, prioritizing areas where disorganization most disrupts your daily routine. Document your observations during this review process. Keeping track of what works well and what doesn't will help you avoid repeating past mistakes. (Sridharan, 2022)

With the insights gained from your annual review, move on to the critical step of setting new goals.

Decluttering objectives should align with both your personal aspirations and the evolving dynamics of your lifestyle. For instance, if you recently transitioned to a remote work situation, your home office may need more focus than before.

Set Specific, Measurable, Achievable, Relevant, and Time-bound (SMART) goals for clarity and direction. These goals could range from organizing the wardrobe to streamlining kitchen storage, based on what's most pressing. Write down each goal, detailing the steps needed to achieve it, similar to creating a project plan. This structure not only keeps you accountable but also breaks down larger tasks into manageable actions. Additionally, it's crucial to involve family members or roommates in this process if applicable, fostering shared accountability and ensuring collective commitment to maintaining order. (Chellappa, 2023)

Once goals are established, the real test lies in adapting your strategies to meet these objectives effectively. Your annual review might reveal that some strategies have outlived their usefulness. Don't shy away from trying new approaches. Perhaps a minimalistic style worked when your schedule was less intense, but now you find yourself needing more functional storage solutions to cater to the quick retrieval of items during your busy mornings.

Consider adopting flexible strategies such as seasonal decluttering, which allows you to rotate items between storage and everyday use according to the season's requirements. You might also benefit from digital tools and apps designed to streamline organizing, especially those geared toward professional busybodies looking for efficient solutions. These can include apps that remind you of periodic cleaning schedules or smart home devices that keep track of belongings.

Moreover, engage in regular check-ins throughout the year to monitor progress and adjust your strategies as needed. Have quarterly mini-reviews where you evaluate specific goals set during the annual planning phase, adapt strategies accordingly, and celebrate smaller milestones. This proactive approach ensures that adjustments happen in real-time, preventing major clutter build-ups. (Sridharan, 2022)

In this journey of continuous improvement, celebrating progress plays a significant role, though it doesn't require formal guidelines. Recognizing accomplishments boosts morale and reinforces positive behavior patterns. After achieving a decluttering milestone, such as reorganizing a room or successfully maintaining order for a set period, reward yourself. Celebrations could be as simple as treating yourself to a favorite activity or sharing your success with others. Tangible acknowledgments of progress instill motivation, making the ongoing process of decluttering feel rewarding rather than burdensome.

Main Points Recap

In this chapter, we've explored how decluttering strategies must adapt to changing circumstances in our lives. The journey toward an organized home is ongoing, especially for busy professionals striving to balance demanding work and personal commitments. Life changes like moving, job shifts, and family dynamics can influence how we manage our spaces and possessions. Recognizing and embracing these changes allows us to refine our approach, ensuring that our surroundings remain aligned with our current lifestyle needs and goals.

Understanding that every individual and situation is unique, the chapter also highlighted the importance of experimenting with different methods until finding one that fits comfortably. Whether it's adjusting decluttering routines seasonally or accommodating emotional attachments to belongings, flexibility is key. By being open to adapting and refining your decluttering strategy, you create a space that not only supports your daily life but also brings peace and efficiency to your home environment.

Reference List

Chellappa, S. (2023, June 27). *Importance of Goal Setting for Employees* . Engagedly. https://engagedly.com/blog/7-reasons-why-goal-setting-is-important/

Iran, S., Cosette Joyner Martinez, & Lisa Sophie Walsleben. (2024, October 1). *Unraveling the Closet: Exploring Reflective Decluttering and its Implications for Long-Term Sufficient Clothing Consumption* . Cleaner and Responsible Consumption; Elsevier BV. https://doi.org/10.1016/j.clrc.2024.100230

Muster, V., Iran, S., & Münsch, M. (2022, August 26). *The cultural practice of decluttering as household work and its potentials for sustainable consumption* . Frontiers in Sustainability. https://doi.org/10.3389/frsus.2022.958538

Sridharan, H. (2022, April 29). *The Impact of Goal Setting on Employee Performance* . Betterworks. https://www.betterworks.com/magazine/impact-of-goal-setting-on-employee-performance/

klock4. (2018, March). *How A Cluttered Home Affects Your Emotions And Your Motherhood* . Motherhood Simplified. https://motherhoodsimplified.com/cluttered-home-affects-emotions-motherhood/

tanner, britnee. (2017, November 9). *Britnee Tanner* . Britnee Tanner. https://britneetanner.com/blog/category/Minimalism

Made in the USA
Columbia, SC
30 January 2025

53001472R00089